OWAC

‖‖ ‖ ‖‖‖‖‖‖‖ ‖ ‖ ‖ ‖‖‖ ‖‖‖‖‖‖‖‖‖‖‖‖‖‖ ‖‖‖ ‖‖‖

W9-CEY-417

Wright Sites

WRIGHT SITES

A Guide to Frank Lloyd Wright Public Places

FOURTH EDITION

**FRANK LLOYD WRIGHT
BUILDING CONSERVANCY**

JOEL HOGLUND,
EDITOR

Princeton Architectural Press, New York

Published by Princeton Architectural Press
A McEvoy Group company
202 Warren Street, Hudson, NY 12534
www.papress.com

 **FRANK LLOYD WRIGHT
BUILDING CONSERVANCY**

ISBN-13: 978-1-61689-577-8

Editors: Abby Bussel, Tom Cho
Designer: Benjamin English

Special thanks to:
Janet Behning, Nolan Boomer, Nicola Brower,
Erin Cain, Barbara Darko, Jenny Florence,
Jan Cigliano Hartman, Lia Hunt, Mia Johnson,
Valerie Kamen, Simone Kaplan-Senchak,
Jennifer Lippert, Kristy Maier, Sara McKay,
Eliana Miller, Rob Shaeffer, Sara Stemen,
Paul Wagner, and Joseph Weston
of Princeton Architectural Press
—Kevin C. Lippert, publisher

Front cover: Hollyhock House, Los Angeles, CA
Back cover: Fallingwater, Mill Run, PA

In celebration of the 150th anniversary of Frank Lloyd Wright's birth, the Frank Lloyd Wright Building Conservancy (the sole organization dedicated to the preservation of all of Wright's extant architecture) is pleased to present the newest edition of *Wright Sites*, a guide to seventy-four structures designed by Wright that are now open to the public.

The growth in the number of publicly accessible sites is a testament to the steady recognition by scholars, architects, and homeowners, among others, of the significance of Wright's contributions to the world's architecture. Diverse in function, style, and material, Wright's designs express a unity of vision—the intimate relationship that must exist between structures and their surroundings in order to be aesthetically satisfying. Additions to the list include the Bachman-Wilson House, recently reconstructed on the grounds of Arkansas's Crystal Bridges Museum of American Art; the Kenneth and Phyllis Laurent House in Rockford, Illinois, Wright's only house designed for a person in a wheelchair; and the Emil and Anna Bach House in Chicago, one of the few publicly accessible Wright houses that accepts overnight guests. In 2016, the R. W. Lindholm House was rescued with the Conservancy's assistance from its threatened site in northern Minnesota and moved to a new location in Pennsylvania, where it will be open to the public in the future.

The Conservancy is of course heartened by the extent of restoration and conservation that has been undertaken since the last edition of this book in 2001. Wright's eminence as an architect cannot realistically stay the effects of time, use, and sometimes misuse upon his work, and the fact that so many endeavor to maintain his buildings provides further proof of Wright's continuing value.

The increased presence of private houses among those open to the public is also well worth noting. While it is true that houses function best as the private residences they were designed to be, occasions for public display arise. We are fortunate that a number of homeowners have bequeathed their houses to the public. Others have adopted a public solution when necessity required that a house be moved from its threatened location. Although no one would find the transformation from private to public to be entirely ideal, since the transformation inevitably eliminates the important personal element of ownership, that fact must be balanced against the undoubted benefits of accessibility. We

8 all gain from the wealth of Wright architecture that is now displayed to the public.

As a final matter, I note that discussion of Wright's significant architectural contribution to Japan has been given equal consideration for the first time in this edition of *Wright Sites*. In that regard, it is instructive to consider the fate of the Imperial Hotel—which "survives" in fragmentary form at the Museum Meiji-Mura after the masterful building was demolished in 1967—and to contrast it with the successful campaign to retain, in central Tokyo, the Jiyu Gakuen School. Collaborative preservation efforts on the local, national, and even international level can prevent the loss of any further Wright structures.

It would not be accurate for the Conservancy to claim credit for all the preservation work illustrated in this volume, which has occurred as the result of the work of many preservation professionals and organizations, together with Wright aficionados and other interested persons. Nonetheless, the Conservancy has, since its founding in 1989, played a significant preservation role at many sites—a role that it continues to play through advocacy, homeowner technical assistance, and programmatic activities, including a yearly conference consisting of scholarly lectures and tours of Wright structures. We welcome your participation in the Conservancy's efforts to save Wright.

Edith K. Payne
President, Board of Directors
Frank Lloyd Wright Building Conservancy

For membership information, contact:

FRANK LLOYD WRIGHT BUILDING CONSERVANCY
53 W. Jackson Blvd., Ste. 1120, Chicago, IL 60604
(312) 663-5500 · preservation@savewright.org

PREFACE

More than fifteen years have passed since the Frank Lloyd Wright Building Conservancy updated this guide to Wright-designed buildings and structures in the United States and Japan that can be visited by the public. In that time, several new sites have been opened for public tours for the first time and changes in ownership have led some Wright houses to return to private use. As a preservation organization first and foremost, the Conservancy recognizes that having Wright houses under the stewardship of preservation-minded owners is the key to their long-term survival; while the public may miss out on seeing a number of remarkable structures, Wright's work is being protected.

Questions of authenticity prompted the removal of other sites that had appeared in earlier editions of *Wright Sites*. The precise extent of Wright's involvement in the Arizona Biltmore, officially credited to architect Albert Chase McArthur, is unclear. Madison's Monona Terrace and the First Christian Church in Scottsdale, constructed from Wright's plans long after his death in 1959, involved changes that lacked the architect's supervision. Even so, these projects remain well worth a visit and are included in our Suggested Itineraries (see page 143). Sites such as the Charnley-Persky House, a product of Wright's time working with Louis Sullivan, and Unity Chapel, a Joseph Silsbee design that Wright contributed to and also referred to as his "first work," are included with acknowledgment of the fact that they are not works solely of Wright's authorship. The decision was made to exclude three Wright-designed medical office buildings—two of which are no longer clinics—that appeared in previous editions, because they are primarily accessible only to clients and patients. Private houses that offer overnight stays to visitors but not regular tours to the public were also excluded. One commercial interior site, the Hoffman Auto Showroom in Manhattan, which appeared in the previous edition, was demolished in 2013—a reminder of the threat facing less iconic, but no less important, Wright designs, especially those located on valuable real estate.

Still, the range of Wright's work open to the public has never been greater. Large Prairie-style mansions, modest homes for the middle class that Wright termed Usonian, an office tower, a vertical research laboratory, a hotel, places of worship, retail shops, a bridge, a gas station, and authentic fragments of lost Wright works fill these pages. The diversity of these sites gives the public a good understanding of the scope and scale of Wright's innovative designs.

10 While many of the sites in this guide operate as house museums with regular tour programs, some still maintain their original function, which we ask all visitors to respect as they encounter neighbors and those who work in these buildings.

As noted in their descriptions, a number of sites require reservations or special arrangements for touring, but visitors to any site should check online and call in advance to confirm availability, as hours may change over time for a variety of reasons, from seasonal closings to restoration projects. Addresses are provided, but please note that some GPS programs may differ in leading drivers to the site, especially in rural areas; obtaining detailed directions when booking a tour is advised.

Please also note that the dates listed in this guide reflect the year of Wright's design, which may differ from the date of completion, and the sites are organized by state and city.

Considerable gratitude is owed to the many dedicated administrators of Wright's public sites, not only for their assistance with revising and updating the contents of this book, but also for their tireless efforts to preserve Wright's work and share it with the public. We must thank the many photographers who have shared their images for this first edition of *Wright Sites* to feature all color photography. The Conservancy also gratefully recognizes Arlene Sanderson, editor of the previous editions of this book, for her role in originating this project when the Conservancy was in its first years of existence. Special thanks go to Scott W. Perkins, chair of the Conservancy's Public Sites committee; John H. Waters, AIA, the Conservancy's preservation programs manager; Jack Quinan, one of the founders of the Conservancy; Karen Severns and Koichi Mori for their assistance with Wright's public sites in Japan; Margo Stipe, curator and registrar of collections at the Frank Lloyd Wright Foundation; and Janet Halstead, executive director of the Frank Lloyd Wright Building Conservancy. On behalf of the community of individuals whose work helps to preserve the architecture of Frank Lloyd Wright, we hope your experiences at these sites inspire, educate, and delight you.

Joel Hoglund, editor
Frank Lloyd Wright Building Conservancy

INTRODUCTION

During the seventy-two years that Frank Lloyd Wright practiced architecture (1887–1959), the United States was transformed by industrial development and massive social change, shifting from a predominantly agrarian to a predominantly urban-industrial society. During that time, Wright designed more than one thousand buildings, roughly five hundred of which were built in more than forty states, Canada, and Japan. Approximately four hundred of these buildings survive today; most are privately held, but the seventy-four cataloged in this book are accessible to the public as house museums or as functioning sites with regular tour programs. *Wright Sites*, a guide to these publicly accessible structures, was first produced by the Frank Lloyd Wright Building Conservancy in 1991 to encourage and facilitate public awareness of and visitations to the sites—and to promote the preservation of all existing Wright architecture.

Public appreciation of Wright's work has grown steadily since his death in 1959, owing to a cluster of intersecting forces. Among them is the demise of the modern movement in architecture, which began around 1910 in Europe, acknowledged Wright as a progenitor, eclipsed him by the 1930s, and faded from view beginning in the '60s. A resurgence of interest in Wright was fostered by the opening of his vast archives to researchers in the early 1980s, the emergence of an ecological consciousness in America—a movement that fits comfortably with Wright's deep regard for nature and the landscape—and the rampant proliferation of truly inferior buildings (merchandising markets, fast-food restaurants, and so-called McMansions) on the American landscape, a phenomenon that fosters an appreciation, if not a hunger, for architecture of real quality. Most important, however, are the buildings themselves, which yield layer upon layer of discovery and pleasure to those who live in them, study them, and visit them.

As a result of these conditions, the market has been flooded with publications on Wright—reproductions of his decorative designs are ubiquitous in museum shops and galleries; exhibitions and symposia occur annually; and documentaries, television series, and even an opera have been written and produced on his life. Most significantly, the number of Wright structures accessible to the public in the United States has risen. Fifty sites were included in the first edition of this book in 1991; seventy-four are included here.

Critics have spoken of Wright not only as America's greatest architect, but as one of the leading creative artists of Western history, along with Michelangelo, Rembrandt, Mozart, and Beethoven. What lies behind this extravagant praise? Is the American view of Wright inflated for chauvinistic reasons, or is his work indeed worthy of such esteem?

The answers can be found in the buildings themselves, as we shall see, but some of the peripheral indicators of Wright's prodigious talent are worth considering. Wright is primarily identified as an architect, but he was also a planner, an engineer, an author and lecturer, an accomplished musician, a social critic, a teacher, a farmer, an avid collector of Asian arts, a photographer, and a prolific designer of furniture and decorative arts. (Much of Wright's earlier work in the form of drawings and documents was lost to fire.)

For many clients, Wright produced a full complement of furniture designs for the commission, each piece unique to the building. The Larkin Administration Building, for instance, included at least thirty-eight distinct furniture designs—five different metal office chairs, five variations on the metal desk, three reclining lounge chairs, three wood-and-leather couches, four wooden chairs, seven different wooden tables, three varieties of lights, an umbrella stand, bookshelves, built-in file cabinets, a barrel chair, etc. Similarly, the Darwin D. Martin House contained more than thirty uniquely designed pieces of furniture. If these two buildings are representative, and if Wright furnished only one-fifth of his buildings, then he would have designed more than two thousand pieces of furniture during his career. This rate of production is especially impressive when one considers that Wright spent most of his career working under considerable duress because he was indifferent to the business side of architecture and his personal life was often in disarray. In addition, for much of the period between 1910 and 1935, owing to personal misfortune and the Great Depression, Wright was hardly able to practice at all. In his final decade, from age 81 to 91, Wright produced six books, traveled widely within the United States and abroad, and realized as many buildings as he had in his previous sixty years!

Nevertheless, architecture, which Wright called "the mother of all the arts," remains central. Wright's architecture occurred in six phases across his career, any one of which would have gained him a distinguished place in American architectural history. His earliest work owes

something to H. H. Richardson, Bruce Price, and McKim, Mead and
White, leading architects of the 1880s whose work was widely published in periodicals. Wright's own Oak Park house, begun in 1889, resembles the shingled American modifications of the Queen Anne style, but its pinwheel plan prefigures recurring spirals throughout Wright's career, culminating with the Solomon R. Guggenheim Museum.

The second phase encompasses the 1890s and is classicizing in nature. The strong if somewhat self-conscious buildings Wright designed during this period (see the Charnley-Persky House of 1891 and Wright's Oak Park studio and library of 1898) frequently include octagons or partial octagons, linear plans, and decorative evidences of Wright's five years under Louis Sullivan.

The third phase, the Prairie period, sometimes referred to as Wright's First Golden Age, began in 1901 and extends into the 1910s. Here Wright created a distinctively American house type (see the Dana-Thomas House, Darwin D. Martin House, Frederick and Lora Robie House, and Meyer and Sophie May House), characterized by strong horizontality, cross-axial planning, low roofs with generous eaves protecting long sequences of art-glass windows, a natural use of materials, skeletal construction, broad openings between rooms, and close attention paid to the siting of the building on the landscape. The Prairie houses were the designs, along with the Larkin Administration Building and Unity Temple, that excited the European modernists. From 1901 to 1909, Wright produced Prairie houses at a rate of about twelve per year.

Wright's interest in the decorative use of a Mayan-inspired vocabulary began in the 1910s (see the A. D. German Warehouse of 1915) and culminated with the Hollyhock House in Los Angeles in 1919. His fifth and most productive period featured the Usonian house (see the Rosenbaum, Loren Pope, Affleck, Laurent, and Bachman-Wilson houses), a lower-cost house type inspired by the housing needs of the Great Depression and World War II. The Usonians employed a heated concrete floor slab, sandwich-wall construction, simplified plan types such as the L-shape and the in-line, and extensive use of built-in furniture, often in plywood. Some of the Usonians are more elaborate, such as the Paul and Jean Hanna House of 1936, and employ hexagonal modules and plans based upon triangles, circles, or hemicircles.

Dana-Thomas House,
interior rendering

overleaf: SC Johnson
Administration Building,
desk and chair drawing

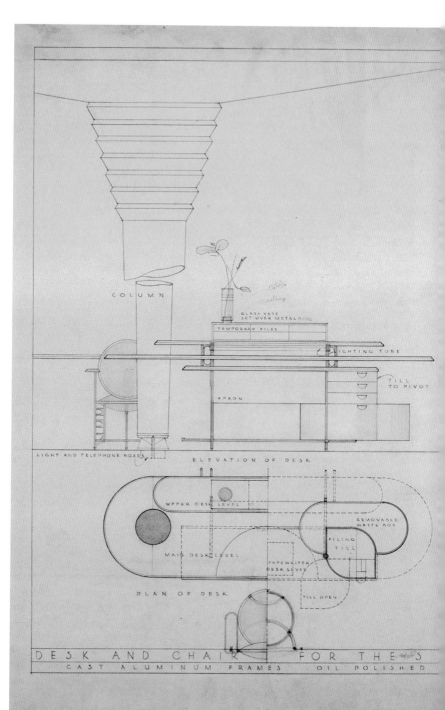

COLUMN

GLASS VASE
SET OVER METAL

TEMPORARY FILES

LIGHTING TUBE

TILL
TO PIVOT

APRON

LIGHT AND TELEPHONE BOXES

ELEVATION OF DESK

UPPER DESK LEVEL

REMOVABLE
WASTE BOX

FILING
TILL

MAIN DESK LEVEL

TYPEWRITER
DESK LEVEL

PLAN OF DESK

TILL OPEN

DESK AND CHAIR FOR THE S
CAST ALUMINUM FRAMES OIL POLISHED

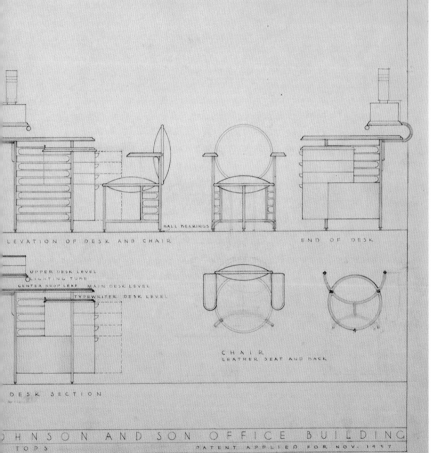

ELEVATION OF DESK AND CHAIR

BALL BEARINGS

END OF DESK

UPPER DESK LEVEL
LIGHTING TUBE
CENTER DROP LEAF   MAIN DESK LEVEL
TYPEWRITER DESK LEVEL

DESK SECTION

CHAIR
LEATHER SEAT AND BACK

JOHNSON AND SON OFFICE BUILDING

TOPS   PATENT APPLIED FOR NOV. 1937

Finally, there are buildings distributed throughout Wright's career, usually large-scale, non-domestic commissions, that are distinguished by the boldness of their conception and the innovativeness of their engineering. These include several extraordinary but demolished structures such as the Larkin Administration Building (1904), Midway Gardens (1914), and the Imperial Hotel, as well as a substantial number of publicly accessible buildings found on these pages, such as Unity Temple, the SC Johnson Administration Building and Research Tower, Florida Southern University, Price Tower, the Solomon R. Guggenheim Museum, the Marin County Civic Center, and Grady Gammage Memorial Auditorium.

All of Wright's work, from the humblest Usonian to the most elaborate Prairie house, is conceived around an idea or grand motif that is expressive of the building's function, its client, and its site, disciplined by elemental geometry. In some instances, such as Hollyhock House or Fallingwater, Wright's title is a clue to the theme of the building. There is good evidence that Wright's manner of creating his buildings was akin to that of the great composers. Indeed, he told one client that he would give him a "domestic symphony," and therein lies the source of endless fascination in Wright's work.

The Frank Lloyd Wright Building Conservancy does not promote and defend Wright's architecture merely because he was prolific and innovative. Rather, it is because these structures were conceived and developed so thoroughly, with such consistency of principle and careful interrelationship of part to part and part to whole as to constitute a composition or thematized system of symphonic pretension, that they endlessly reward those who wish to engage them.

Jack Quinan
Distinguished Professor of Art History Emeritus
State University of New York, Buffalo
Founding Director, Frank Lloyd Wright Building Conservancy

Stanley and Mildred Rosenbaum House

1939

601 Riverview Dr.
Florence, AL 35630
(256) 718-5050

wrightinalabama.com

"The house of moderate cost is not only America's major architectural problem but the problem most difficult for her major architects," Frank Lloyd Wright wrote in his 1943 autobiography. Wright spent much of the latter part of his career answering that challenge with his functional, cost-effective Usonian houses.

By omitting a basement and attic, embedding heating pipes in a concrete floor mat, centralizing the mechanical systems and plumbing near the kitchen, and building in furnishings and lighting, Wright intended to develop a simpler, more efficient house suited to the informality of middle-American family life. His concept anticipated the prefabrication of major building components. The walls, for example, were designed with a plywood core sandwiched between board-and-batten interior and exterior surfaces. Conventional framing, plaster, and paint were thus eliminated.

A pure example of the Usonian type, the Rosenbaum House was designed as a 1,540-square-foot, L-shaped plan on a two-by-four-foot grid, built at a cost of $12,000. The large living room includes an asymmetrically positioned fireplace and dining alcove at one end and a one-hundred-square-foot study at the other. The bedroom wing provided

access to three rooms off a long, narrow gallery lined with bookshelves and storage. In 1948, Wright designed a significant addition to the house, adding 1,084 square feet and providing a larger kitchen, a playroom, and guest quarters that wrap three sides of a landscaped courtyard.

Tidewater cypress and red brick made from local northern Alabama clay combine to establish a nearly solid wall on the street side of the house. The twenty-foot-long cantilevered carport reinforces the house's emphatic horizontal profile. By contrast, the rear of the house is open to the surrounding landscape, with floor-to-ceiling windows and glazed doors that reveal the terrace, a Japanese garden, and the woods beyond.

The fretwork plywood panels framing the clerestory windows and concealing recessed lights are typical of Usonian houses and are consistent with Wright's philosophy of integral ornament. Original Wright-designed furnishings and reproductions of the original dining room chairs are supplemented by pieces by Charles and Ray Eames.

The house underwent a complete restoration and was opened as a city-owned museum in 2002. A new gift shop was added in 2014.

Taliesin West

Begun 1938

12345 N. Taliesin Dr.
Scottsdale, AZ 85258
(480) 627-5340

franklloydwright.org

In 1937, Frank Lloyd Wright purchased six hundred acres of rugged land in the Sonoran Desert at the foot of Arizona's McDowell Mountain. Here he established an experimental desert camp that would serve as his winter home, studio, and architectural laboratory until his death in 1959. Over the years, the complex was continually altered and expanded to comprise a drafting studio, Wright's office and private living quarters, dining facilities, three theaters, and a workshop, as well as residences for apprentices and staff, all situated among pools, terraces, and gardens.

Constructed of stone, cement, redwood, and canvas, the buildings seem to grow out of the desert terrain that inspired their design. Their angled roofs, exposed beams, and rubble walls mirror the colors, textures, and forms of the surrounding landscape. As the buildings took on greater permanence, steel and fiberglass replaced the less durable materials.

The ninety-six-by-thirty-foot drafting room with a fireplace and desert masonry vault, a communal dining room, and two apartments form the core of the complex. An adjoining terrace leads to the fifty-six-foot-long garden room with a sloping, translucent roof and a fireplace. Wright's private quarters were located in the wing extending at a ninety-degree

angle to the southeast. Additional structures (the Cabaret Theater and a larger pavilion for live performances, concerts, and lectures) were designed to house social and cultural activities integrated into the educational program of the Taliesin Fellowship and Frank Lloyd Wright School of Architecture. Apprentices live in apartments on the site, as well as in shelters they construct of their own designs scattered throughout the surrounding desert.

Taliesin West is the international headquarters of the Frank Lloyd Wright Foundation, which owns and manages Taliesin West as well as Taliesin in Spring Green, Wisconsin.

ASU Gammage

Grady Gammage Memorial Auditorium

1959

1200 S. Forest Ave.
Tempe, AZ 85281
(480) 965-5062

asugammage.com

During the last year of his life, Frank Lloyd Wright received his only civic commission from the state of Arizona, where he lived during the winter months. This final Wright-designed public space is a circular performing arts center with a three-thousand-seat auditorium, classrooms, and offices. It was based on Wright's Baghdad Opera House, one of a series of unrealized structures designed by the architect in 1957 as part of his Plan for Greater Baghdad.

The auditorium, commissioned by Grady Gammage, Arizona State University's ninth president and a longtime friend of the architect, sits on a fifteen-acre site on the southwest corner of the campus. Wright designed two two-hundred-foot-long pedestrian bridges that rise from the adjacent lawn and sunken parking area to the circular building. Constructed of steel, cast concrete, and brick, the building cost $2.5 million.

An arcade of fifty fifty-five-foot-tall columns wraps the facade, framing the glass-walled lobby and supporting the outer edge of the thin-shell concrete roof. The plan is divided into two circles of unequal size. The larger contains the promenades, lobbies, and audience hall; the smaller, the stage, dressing rooms, workshops, classrooms, and offices.

Patrons enter and exit the auditorium's continental-style seating area through twenty-four doors along the sides and rear of the hall. A grand tier and balcony provide upper-level seating. The grand tier, supported by a 145-foot-long girder, is detached from the rear wall, allowing sound to encircle the audience.

The 140-foot-wide proscenium stage is readily adaptable to a wide range of theatrical productions, symphony concerts, chamber music recitals, and lectures. The steel acoustical shell can be mechanically adjusted to accommodate a full symphony orchestra and choir, or collapsed against the rear wall.

Neither Wright nor Gammage lived to see the building completed in 1964. William Wesley Peters of Taliesin Associated Architects was responsible for the engineering and much of the interior design of the building.

The building may be visited during scheduled performances, and tours are available by appointment.

Bachman-Wilson House

Gloria Bachman and Abraham Wilson House

1954

600 Museum Way
Bentonville, AR 72712
(479) 418-5700

crystalbridges.org

Gloria Bachman and her husband, Abraham Wilson, commissioned Wright to design their Usonian house in Millstone, New Jersey, in 1953. Lawrence and Sharon Tarantino, an architecture and design team, purchased the house in 1988 and restored it, but over their twenty-five years of ownership, the site along the Millstone River was subject to increasingly frequent and intense flooding that threatened to destroy the house. In 2012 they concluded that saving the house required relocating it—and after extensive study, the Frank Lloyd Wright Building Conservancy agreed. Unable to find a local buyer, the owners began an international search for a patron with an appropriate site and resources.

In January 2014, Crystal Bridges Museum of American Art announced it had acquired the house and would move it to the museum grounds. The Philippine mahogany architectural building components, including the board-and-batten walls and the ceiling, doors, windows, built-ins, and all of the house's furnishings, were labeled, packed, and loaded onto two container trucks for the 1,235-mile journey to northwest Arkansas. The house's new site overlooks the native woodlands and Crystal Spring—a natural spring that provides freshwater for the flora and fauna of the Crystal Bridges grounds—near the south entrance

of the Moshe Safdie–designed museum. A basement was added to facilitate a commercial-sized HVAC system, and a new foundation slab and concrete blocks were built to 1954 specifications with materials available during that time.

The elongated, two-story structure has a mezzanine overlooking the living room and a guest bedroom on the main level. Two more bedrooms, each with a cantilevered outdoor balcony, are accessed from the mezzanine level, with a guest bedroom on the main floor. Unique features include the triple band of perforated clerestory panels with the Samara design and an eleven-foot-high, sixty-foot-long concrete-block wall that extends across the front of the house to add privacy. Built-in seating in the living room faces a wall of ten-foot windows and doors that open onto the backyard and forest.

Students and faculty at the Fay Jones School of Architecture and Design in nearby Fayetteville designed and constructed an interpretive pavilion for the grounds of the house. The Bachman-Wilson House and the pavilion opened to the public in November 2015.

Anderton Court Shops

1952

Frank Lloyd Wright's only retail space built in Southern California sits on fashionable Rodeo Drive. Six boutiques across three floors are arranged around a central light well and connected by ramps that wrap around a central pylon. A separate unit on the third floor was designed as a penthouse apartment with a large living and dining space, two bedrooms, a fireplace, and a studio space above, but it was later converted to office space.

The building is 150 feet deep with 50 feet of west-facing frontage. Wright designed the facade as an inverted V to enable greater street exposure on the prime piece of real estate. The central stylized pylon reaches well beyond the rooftop, commanding the attention of street traffic. Downward tapering piers, fascia, and soffit detailing all echo the chevron pattern created in the central spire, roofline, and angled walkway ramps.

As an active retail development, the building has undergone changes inconsistent with Wright's original design, but the overall integrity of the landmarked structure remains intact. There are no organized tours, but shops can be visited during retail hours.

4808 Hollywood Blvd.
Los Angeles, CA 90027
(323) 913-4030
barnsdall.org/
hollyhock-house

Hollyhock House ■

Aline Barnsdall House

1919

Variously described as Mayan, pre-Columbian, Asian, and even Egyptian, the large and enigmatic house Frank Lloyd Wright designed for oil heiress and theatrical producer Aline Barnsdall defies stylistic categorization. It is a transitional structure, a bridge between Wright's Prairie houses of the preceding decades and the textile-block houses to come.

Barnsdall commissioned Wright to design an elaborate complex of residences, theaters, shops, and apartments to serve a Los Angeles community of avant-garde artists. Hollyhock House (Barnsdall's private residence), two guest residences, and a springhouse were the only buildings to be completed. A structure known as the Little Dipper was begun but never completed; its retaining walls remain.

Initial plans to construct the house out of reinforced concrete were abandoned, and construction proceeded in hollow tile, stucco, and wood. Hollyhocks, Barnsdall's favorite flower, inspired the cast-concrete ornamental bands on the exterior walls, as well as the capitals on the courtyard piers and the finials projecting from the roof.

The quadrangular plan encloses a large garden court that terminates in a circular pool. The central block of the house comprises an entry loggia and a living room, which is flanked by a library and music room.

Two opposing wings, which extend from the main living area, contain the bedrooms, dining room, and service areas of the home. The living room is distinguished by a central fireplace with a decorative overmantel and projecting hearth surrounded by a pool of water. Barnsdall's wish for a residence that was half house and half garden is answered in numerous terraces, colonnades, and pergolas that join the interior spaces with the garden.

In 1927, Barnsdall donated Hollyhock House, one of the guest residences, and twelve acres of what is now Barnsdall Art Park to the City of Los Angeles. In 1974, Lloyd Wright, Frank Lloyd Wright's son, directed a restoration of the house. In 1991, its massive living room seating group was reconstructed using historic photographs. Following a three-year restoration that included extensive roof repair, new drains, and a meticulous recreation of architectural details in the primary interior rooms, Hollyhock House reopened in 2014.

Pilgrim Congregational Church ■
1958

In 1958, while Frank Lloyd Wright was working on the Solomon R. Guggenheim Museum, he accepted a commission from a fledgling church in Redding, California—at the time a small town of twelve thousand residents. The committee that was formed to realize the congregation's own house of worship had such a long list of wants, the congregation's twenty-seven-year-old minister, Ray Welles, joked they may need to enlist Frank Lloyd Wright. The chairman of the committee, an architect, decided to cold-call Wright, and some weeks later they received word back: "Tell the little church I'll help them out."

Wright invited the young minister to Taliesin West to present the designs, which, according to church historians, Wright referred to as "pole and boulder gothic" and said represented the form of a tent as a symbol of temporary and transient lives. Wright's master plan shows the main sanctuary facing down a sloping hill, with a small chapel on one side and administration offices and a library on the other. Another wing contained a fellowship hall, classrooms, and a nursery. After Wright died in 1959, Taliesin Associated Architects oversaw final construction of the planned fellowship hall as the main sanctuary of the church. The remainder of Wright's plan was not constructed. Parishioners and volunteers from the community completed most of the construction using more than ninety tons of rock. Reinforced concrete replaced the redwood trusses Wright intended to support the roof.

The church holds regular public services and may be viewed during regular office hours.

V. C. Morris Gift Shop

1948

140 Maiden Ln.
San Francisco, CA 94108

CALIFORNIA

In his redesign of an existing building into a gift shop for California businessman V. C. Morris, Frank Lloyd Wright rejected all conventions of ground-level display windows used for retail establishments. The street side of the building is an imposing masonry facade with a dramatic archway that recalls the influence of Louis Sullivan, Wright's early employer and teacher. The solid brick wall is pierced by a tall, thin strip of glass and a series of illuminated glass blocks. The composition is an elegantly conceived interplay of solid and void, light and shadow, angle and curve.

Wright intended the mysterious reticence of the facade to entice passersby through the tunnel-like entrance to the interior, which is an expansive, light-filled space well suited to the display of art and decorative wares. A curvilinear ramp leads to the upper level and provides additional display area along its path. The ramp walls contain circular recesses for the display of art, as well as openings that offer views to the other levels of the store. The curvilinear theme extends to the custom black-walnut display cases, tables, seating, and built-in cabinetry included in Wright's designs for the space. Similarities between the design of the store and Wright's concurrent work on plans for the Solomon R. Guggenheim Museum are obvious.

Occupied by successive retailers after Morris's death, the building was purchased in 1997 by the owners of Xanadu Gallery, who undertook necessary restoration work. The gallery of art and antiquities is now closed, and the building was acquired for retail leasing by a new owner in 2015. In late 2016, plans were in place to reopen the building with a high-end fashion retailer.

Marin County Civic Center

1957

3501 Civic Center Dr.
San Rafael, CA 94903
(415) 473-3762

marincounty.org/
depts/cu/tours

34

CALIFORNIA

In 1957, the Marin County Board of Supervisors commissioned Frank Lloyd Wright to develop a master plan for a 140-acre site north of downtown San Rafael. Wright designed the master plan and preliminary plans for the Administration Building and Hall of Justice in 1957. He presented the design to Marin County in late March 1958, and preliminary plans for a theater, an auditorium, a fairground pavilion, and a lagoon were completed later that year. After Wright's death in 1959, Wright associates William Wesley Peters and Aaron Green took over as project directors.

Wright's plan specified a 584-foot-long Administration Building and an 880-foot-long Hall of Justice that would bridge the valleys between three adjacent hills. The two wings meet at a flattened dome, 80 feet in diameter and accented by a 172-foot-tall gold-colored tower encasing a smokestack. The Administration Building houses offices as well as a circular county library and the Anne T. Kent California Room. The Hall of Justice, completed in 1969, contains offices, a cafe, the original county jail, and circular courtrooms.

Wright planned the building's central atriums to be open to the sky, but practical considerations prompted a change to barrel-vaulted skylights after his death. The exterior screen walls are divided into rhythmic arcades and circular openings that shade the buildings' interiors while framing views of the surrounding hills. The circular motif is continued in the grillwork and gold-anodized aluminum spheres rimming the roof edge.

The buildings were constructed of precast, prestressed concrete and steel. Segmentation and the use of expansion joints allow the buildings to withstand seismic shock. The site includes a post office, the only Wright-designed US government facility ever constructed. Later additions to the site include the two-thousand-seat Marin Veterans' Memorial Auditorium, a 22,500-square-foot exhibition hall, fairgrounds, and a maintenance facility, which were not of Wright's design.

Paul and Jean Hanna House

1936

737 Frenchmans Rd.
Stanford, CA 94305
(650) 725-8352

hannahousetours
.stanford.edu

This house, designed for a Stanford University professor and his young family, exemplifies Frank Lloyd Wright's endless exploration and innovation. For the first time, abandoning the square or rectangle in favor of the hexagon as a basic unit for the grid and plan, Wright found a new freedom that translated into a remarkable degree of flexibility and spatial continuity. Walls joined at 120 degrees create an interior of fluid space and unrestricted views, further extended by large expanses of glass that open out to the terraces and hillside. Given its hexagonal grid, the house was nicknamed the Honeycomb House.

Even in its initial design, the house greatly exceeded the Hannas' proposed budget of $15,000, and continued to grow through successive additions to encompass 4,825 square feet. In 1950 the Hannas added a wing, separated from the main house by the carport, that included guest quarters and a workshop. In 1957 they again turned to Wright, asking him to remodel the three children's bedrooms into a new master bedroom and to convert the original into a library/office.

While generally considered a Usonian, the eventual size and cost of this dwelling far surpassed the means of the typical Middle American. But the reliance on a grid in the development of the plan, interior and

exterior board-and-batten walls, and central location of the kitchen are characteristics shared with Wright's Usonian designs elsewhere.

The Hannas' published correspondence with the architect demonstrates their shared commitment to achieving a house that would respond to the changing needs of family life while embodying Wright's principles of organic design. This partnership challenged the resources of architect and client alike to produce a dwelling of enduring appeal.

In 2000, a restoration was completed by Stanford University, the owner of the house, which operates tours by appointment.

Florida Southern College

Begun 1938

750 Frank Lloyd Wright Way
Lakeland, FL 33803
(863) 680-4597

flsouthern.edu/visitors/
fllw-visitors.aspx

In 1938, Dr. Ludd Spivey, president of Florida Southern College from 1925 to 1957, telegrammed Frank Lloyd Wright at Taliesin to engage him in designing a "great education temple in Florida." At the time of the commission, Spivey envisioned a chapel, a library, an administration building, faculty housing, dormitories, classrooms, an industrial arts building, a music building, a science and cosmography building, and an art gallery with studio workshops. Today, the Florida Southern College Historic District is the largest single-site collection of Wright architecture in the world.

Over the next twenty years, buildings of Wright's design took form, beginning in 1938 with the hexagonal Annie Pfeiffer Chapel, which is both the tallest building of the complex and the focal point of the plan. The chapel's angular, vertical silhouette provides a strong visual counterpoint to the low, flat-roofed, rectangular seminar buildings of 1940 and the circular reading room of the original Roux Library, completed in 1945. Other Wright-designed structures are the Emile E. Watson and Benjamin Fine Administration Buildings (completed in 1948), two buildings separated by a courtyard containing a reflecting pool and connected by an esplanade; the Lucius Pond Ordway Building (completed in 1952), with interior courtyards and a circular theater; the small William

H. Danforth Chapel (completed in 1955); and the three-story Polk County Science Building (completed in 1958), which contains the only planetarium of Wright's design.

The walls and structural members of the buildings are uniformly constructed of reinforced, textile-block walls. Wright's philosophy of integral ornament is demonstrated in the contrasting surfaces of smooth, textured, and perforated blocks, and the abstract patterns of colored glass set into the concrete for decorative effect. Covered esplanades link the collection of Wright-designed buildings. He intended the trellises that extend from the copper-trimmed roofs to support trailing vines. The light wells and large planters along the flat-roofed walkways, in addition to the trees preserved from the orange grove that originally occupied the land, create a gardenlike setting on the eighty-acre site.

Over the past decade more than $8 million has been spent to restore many of the structures, including the interior of the Annie Pfeiffer Chapel, the windows in both chapels and the administration buildings, the esplanades, the circular theater, and the Water Dome fountain. In 2013 a previously unbuilt Wright design for Usonian-style faculty housing was constructed as the centerpiece of a new Visitors Center.

Spring House

Clifton and George Lewis House

1952

3117 Okeeheepkee Rd.
Tallahassee, FL 32303

preservespringhouse.org

Located on five wooded acres on the outskirts of Tallahassee, Spring House (named for the natural spring on the property) is the only private house designed by Frank Lloyd Wright to be built in Florida. George Lewis and his wife, Clifton, approached Wright to design their house after attending a conference in 1950 at the Wright-designed Florida Southern College campus. Construction was completed by the end of 1954. Some exterior features, such as the terrace wall and reflecting pool, were not built.

Spring House is one of only eleven houses Wright realized in the hemicycle style, a form characterized by curved and glazed walls that he developed late in his career. It is one of only two hemicycle houses with an unusual boatlike shape. The construction material is Ocala block—a type of concrete block popular in midcentury Florida that aggregates limestone mined from Ocala, Florida, in the mix, producing a distinctive range of colors—with tidewater red cypress siding on the exterior and interior mezzanine. The ground floor contains a circular workspace and two-story living space with full-height windows looking out onto the woods. The curving mezzanine hallway overlooking the living space connects three bedrooms, two bathrooms, and balconies at both ends of the house.

The Lewis family lived in Spring House until 2010. Clifton Lewis founded the nonprofit Spring House Institute to restore and complete the house, now also known as the Lewis Spring House, according to Wright's original plans. The Institute conducts a monthly open house tour and arranges personal tours at other times with reservations.

Belvidere Cemetery
E. Harrison St. at Webster St.
Belvidere, IL 61008
(815) 547-7642

Pettit Memorial Chapel

1906

Emma Glasner Pettit commissioned Frank Lloyd Wright to design a chapel for the Belvidere Cemetery as a memorial to her husband, Dr. William H. Pettit. At the time of his death in 1899, Pettit lived and practiced in Cedar Falls, Iowa, but he had grown up in Belvidere, Illinois. Mrs. Pettit was introduced to Wright's work when he designed a house in Glencoe, Illinois, for Mrs. Pettit's brother William Glasner in 1905.

This small, chaste, Prairie-period structure has a cruciform plan that terminates in lateral porches providing protected access and extending the usable space. Features typical of Wright's Prairie designs include the hipped roof, broad eaves, bands of art-glass windows, horizontal wood trim, and central brick fireplace.

The stucco building, which cost $3,000 to construct, was restored in 1981 with $56,000 in funds raised by the local Junior Woman's Club. The windows were recreated from original drawings and photographs, and the light fixtures and ceiling trim were inspired by similar Wright designs of the period. There are no regular tours of the building's interior, but visitors who arrive during the cemetery's open hours may call management at the phone number posted on the door to request access to the chapel.

Charnley-Persky House

James and Helen Charnley House

1891

1365 N. Astor St.
Chicago, IL 60610
(312) 573-1365

charnleyhouse.org

Frank Lloyd Wright, at the age of twenty-four, was the chief draftsman in the office of Dankmar Adler and Louis Sullivan when James Charnley commissioned the design of this Chicago house. The firm specialized in large commercial structures, so smaller residential commissions were often assigned to Wright. Research indicates that Sullivan, a personal friend of the Charnley family, sketched out the basic symmetrical plan of the house then turned the project over to Wright to detail the interiors, ornament, and materials. The house is the product of their collaboration.

In the design of the Charnley-Persky House, Wright said he first recognized the decorative value of the plain surface. The uncompromising simplicity, boldly stated geometry, and decorative restraint of the building's exterior distinguished it from other turn-of-the-century residences in Chicago's prestigious Gold Coast neighborhood. Taking a design cue from Sullivan's skyscrapers of the period, the facade is divided into three clearly differentiated, interlocking parts: the dressed-stone base extends to frame the entrance, the two-story block of Roman brick recedes to frame a central loggia, and a thin stringcourse of contrasting stone delineates the attic floor.

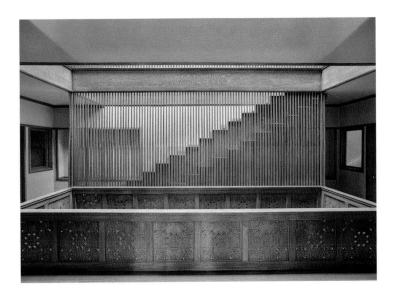

The interior plan is equally straightforward. A dramatic open stairhall rises three floors to a central skylight. The large entrance hall dominates the center of the first-floor space with the living and dining rooms on opposite ends. Bedrooms are located on the second floor, servants' quarters on the third, and the kitchen and laundry in the basement. Sullivan's influence is noticeable in the symmetrical plan and the carved decorative detailing on the wood mantels and trim throughout the house. Wright's hand can be seen in the building's flat decorative panels and the screen of tapered balusters that both separate and reveal the staircase leading to the third floor.

The building has undergone many renovations and restorations, including the replacement of the deteriorated balcony in the 1970s and a restoration by Skidmore, Owings & Merrill in 1988, which included the demolition of a 1920s addition. Currently, the house serves as the national headquarters of the Society of Architectural Historians.

Emil and Anna Bach House

1915

7415 N. Sheridan Rd.
Chicago, IL 60626
tours: (312) 994-4000
rentals: (773) 654-3959

emilbachhouse.com

Frank Lloyd Wright designed this compact two-story house near the coast of Lake Michigan for Emil Bach, the owner (along with his five brothers) of Chicago's Bach Brick Company. A few years prior, in 1912, Emil's brother Otto had purchased the Oscar M. Steffens House, a Wright-designed Prairie house built two blocks to the north in 1908 (and since demolished).

At the time of its construction, the Bach House had an unobstructed view east to the lake. Guests approach the east-facing entrance from the south and experience the geometric, cubic massing and overhanging flats roofs of the house from multiple angles on a circuitous route to the entry door. The square first floor is arranged around a central brick fireplace with an adjacent inglenook created by a built-in bench and a partially built-in dining table projecting outward from the hearth into the living space. Upstairs are three bedrooms and two bathrooms, one of which was converted from the former servant's room. Unlike the lower-level windows, which are inset to provide privacy from the street, the upper-level bay windows are cantilevered outward. An open porch with a sundeck above it originally looked out toward the lake, but as density in the urban area increased in the 1920s and multifamily apartment

buildings sprang up between the Bach House and the shore, these spaces were enclosed. Subsequent owners also removed the original art-glass windows.

In 2009, after ten different owners, the Bach House was acquired by Tawani Enterprises and underwent an extensive two-year restoration to return the house more closely to its 1915 appearance. The original art-glass windows were reproduced, and the open porch and sundeck were restored. A pool house built by a subsequent owner at the rear of the property was adapted to a contemporary Japanese-style teahouse. Since 2014 the house has been rented as an event space (up to seventy-five guests can be accommodated in the house and gardens) and for overnight stays. The Frank Lloyd Wright Trust also conducts regular guided tours.

Frederick and Lora Robie House

1909

5757 S. Woodlawn Ave.
Chicago, IL 60637

flwright.org/visit/
robiehouse

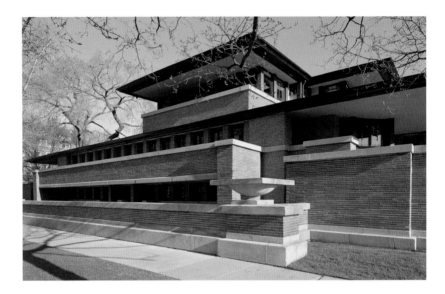

The Robie House remains Frank Lloyd Wright's consummate Prairie-style house adapted to an urban site. A distinctive presence in this neighborhood of large, turn-of-the-century houses and eclectic university buildings, this long, low dwelling with its dramatic twenty-foot-long, cantilevered terrace roofs still seems a structural marvel.

Frederick Robie was a successful bicycle manufacturer as well as an engineer and aspiring automobile designer. According to Robie, he sketched his own idea of what a house should be and passed the design among a few builders. "You want one of those damn Wright houses," he was told.

The house Wright designed both satisfied his client and fully integrated the design elements developed in earlier Prairie residences. Wright eliminated the basement and set the building on a concrete water table. Brick piers and steel beams provide the structural framework upon which the three graduated tiers of the house rest. The low, hipped roof with its wide and projecting eaves and the narrow brick with raked, horizontal mortar joints reinforce the dominant horizontality of the building.

The entrance is concealed on the north side of the building. The first floor contains a playroom, a billiard room, and an attached garage. Robie

shared Wright's fascination with the automobile, which may explain the three-car garage outfitted with an engine pit and car wash. The main living area is located on the second floor; the long, open expanse of space on this level is interrupted only by the fireplace block separating the dining and living room areas. The third-floor bedrooms include a master suite with a fireplace and bath. At each level, doors and windows open onto terraces, balconies, or porches, extending the living space out into nature. Lacking sufficient ground for a garden, Wright carried the landscaping aloft in massive planters and urns, whose trailing foliage softened the dense mass of the exterior walls.

Wright designed the house in its entirety, enriching the interior with furnishings, light fixtures, rugs, and art glass. The house, including the lot, cost Robie $59,000, a considerable sum at the time. The sale of the house in 1911, just two years after completion, coincided with the failure of Robie's marriage and business. In 1957, the building was saved from demolition by a realty company that later transferred ownership to the University of Chicago. Since then, restoration work has been ongoing.

Rookery Building Alterations

1905

209 S. LaSalle St.
Chicago, IL 60604
(312) 994-4000

flwright.org/visit/
rookery

Frank Lloyd Wright was no stranger to the design of Chicago's largest and most expensive office building of the late 1880s, the Rookery. The ten-story structure, designed by Daniel H. Burnham and John W. Root, housed the offices of Wright's clients William Winslow and the Luxfer Prism Company. Wright himself maintained an office in the building from 1898 to 1899, although he continued to design primarily from his suburban studio in Oak Park. In 1905 Edward C. Waller, the building's manager and another of Wright's clients, commissioned the architect to remodel the entrance and first-floor public areas of the Rookery.

Wright's design entailed refacing the walls of the Adams Street and LaSalle Street lobbies and encasing the intricate metalwork of columns in the central light court with white marble, unifying these three large first-floor spaces. The incised and gilded relief of the marble panels that line the walls of each lobby reflects Wright's own interpretation of Root's ornamental schemes elsewhere in the building. Wright designed the suspended geometric light fixtures, replacing the large electroliers on the courtyard stairways with marble urns of similar scale. Around 1930, a second remodeling was undertaken by William Drummond, a former Wright apprentice. Drummond's work is represented in the design of the entrance doors and the LaSalle Street elevator lobby.

First National Bank of Dwight

122 W. Main St.
Dwight, IL 60420
(815) 584-1212

Frank L. Smith Bank Building

1905

The simple dignity and solidity of the cut-stone facade of the First National Bank of Dwight, prominently situated on a small-town main street, is consistent with Frank Lloyd Wright's belief that banks should express their own character rather than resemble temples of worship. His view was surely influenced by his mentor, Louis Sullivan, who first denounced the Roman temples that housed many banking enterprises. Independently, the two architects produced highly original solutions to the design of the Midwestern bank building.

Wright's early drawing of "A Village Bank," published in a 1901 issue of *Brickbuilder* magazine, and his later design of the Smith Bank deliberately reject classical or historical references. A 1904 drawing documents an earlier design for the Smith Bank that shows a vertical brick block with two columns flanking a recessed central entrance and a wide ornamental frieze on the upper level of the facade, but this scheme was abandoned.

The plan of the square building, as constructed, is as simple and forthright as its stone exterior. A central entrance divides the public space into a banking room on one side and a main office on the other. Space for three offices was reserved at the rear of the building. The walls are trimmed with narrow wood strips in a spare geometric pattern. Originally, a large skylight provided natural light and ventilation. A 1991 remodeling and addition closely approximate the character and materials of the original structure. This project restored much of the bank's integrity diminished through earlier alterations.

No tours are conducted, but the building is open during regular bank hours.

2001 S. Batavia Ave.
Geneva, IL 60134
(630) 377-6424

ppfv.org

Fabyan Villa ■

George and Nelle Fabyan House

1907

Owing to the constraints of this commission, the home Frank Lloyd Wright designed for wealthy textile merchant George Fabyan and his wife, Nelle, for what was to become a 350-acre estate on the Fox River, contrasts with his typical Prairie-period work.

Incorporated into the north and west sections of the cruciform plan is an earlier L-shaped structure, which probably dictated the clapboard siding and gable roof used in the construction. The shape of the roof is reflected in the second-story windows and the polygonal motif on the concrete piers. Wright added a two-story bedroom wing to the south, upper- and lower-level porches to the east, three verandas, and a courtyard screen fence. These ground-level, exterior structures visually balance the massive, heavily banded stucco eaves. The six-thousand-square-foot house contains four fireplaces of varied construction. The millwork is consistent with that found in Wright's Prairie houses. The pantry and first-floor bath are intact, along with a number of custom-made furnishings. Both the villa and the large estate on which it sits, Riverbank, with its Japanese garden and Dutch windmill, document the varied interests of the clients, which included cryptology, Asian art, acoustics, and horticulture.

Since 1940 the home and estate have been owned by the Forest Preserve District of Kane County. Since 1995, Preservation Partners of the Fox Valley has managed the house museum operations for the district in partnership with Friends of Fabyan, a volunteer group. The district has undertaken many preservation and restoration projects on the property. The house is open seasonally for tours.

Ravine Bluffs Bridge Reconstruction and Sculptures

1915

Sylvan Rd. west of Franklin Rd.
Glencoe, IL, 60022

wrightinglencoe.org

In 1911 Frank Lloyd Wright designed an elaborate estate for his attorney, Sherman Booth, with a bridge drive spanning a ravine and leading to the house and grounds. Following the construction of the stables and dual garage/gardener's quarters in 1912 and a summer cottage in 1913, the estate's original design was modified in 1914 due to higher than expected construction costs and an economic downturn. The redesigned house incorporated the stables and garage, while the estate's land was transformed into Ravine Bluffs, a suburban development of twenty-three lots.

Five other Wright-designed houses—still private residences, but viewable from the street—were constructed at Ravine Bluffs in 1915. The bridge design was modified slightly and located to serve as a city street. Originally, the bridge contained an opening in the deck near a seating alcove at the center to allow for a mature tree to pass through. Wright designed the low sculptural square urns and rectangular light pillars found at each end of the bridge as well as the three recently restored sculptures at the subdivision entrances.

After serious structural deterioration, the bridge was precisely reconstructed in 1985 with an exact replica. The reinforced concrete deck of the three-span bridge is supported by three-foot-wide piers. The center span has an inaccessible mezzanine located between the deck and floor of the ravine. The bridge accommodates a one-lane road and a pedestrian walkway with a semicircular seating area. A Wright-designed railroad waiting station once stood near the south entrance to Ravine Bluffs. The structure was demolished in the 1950s, but the Glencoe Historical Society is working to build a replica on the original site.

B. Harley and Anna ■
Bradley House

1900

In 1900, Frank Lloyd Wright designed two adjacent houses for businessman B. Harley Bradley and his brother-in-law, Warren Hickox Jr., on the banks of the Kankakee River. (The Hickox House remains in private hands.) The features of the Bradley House would come to characterize Wright's mature Prairie-style buildings.

The building has a cruciform plan, with the living room and kitchen on the main axis, the dining room and reception room on the cross axis, and a large central fireplace at the intersection. The main entrance can be found beneath a broad carriage porch on the north facade. A half-octagonal bay window in the east wall of the living room leads to an outdoor terrace surrounded by a waist-high wall. South of the living room is a large corner porch overlooking the river. On the second floor there are four primary bedrooms plus two servants' quarters. The master bedroom shares a window extension above the large bay window in the living room below.

The low-pitched cross-gable roofs with large overhangs protect ribbons of leaded-glass casement windows and exaggerate the horizontality of the house. The gable ends cant slightly upward, adding a subtle Japanese element—the only design feature taken from a foreign influence.

Instead of the heavy masonry used in his earlier houses, Wright used lighter wood-stud construction sheathed in stucco. The stucco, trimmed with dark wood accents, unifies the wings and emphasizes the flat lines of the prairie in the six-thousand-square-foot main house, the two-story stable at the rear of the property, and the open breezeway connecting them. Wright called the accents "the expressive flow of continuous surface."

The Bradleys left Kankakee in 1913, after which the house changed hands several times. In the mid-1950s, it was converted to a restaurant (a commercial kitchen on the south side of the breezeway was added and later removed). After thirty years as the destination restaurant Yesteryear, the building was repurposed again, this time as offices. In 2005, it was purchased by a local couple who undertook a five-year restoration. It is now owned by the nonprofit Wright in Kankakee and operated as a house museum.

Francisco Terrace Apartments Archway Reconstruction

1895

In 1895, Frank Lloyd Wright designed a two-story apartment building—Francisco Terrace—intended to house the working-class residents of what was then Chicago's Near West Side. The client, Edward C. Waller, was an important early patron of Wright's whose many grand proposals included social planning for the working poor.

The original forty-four-unit building was designed around a large rectangular central courtyard. Although stair towers were located at the corners of the building block, each unit was also independently accessible from either the street or the courtyard. After years of neglect, Francisco Terrace was demolished in 1974, despite attempts by local preservationists to save the structure. The archway, all cut stone, terra-cotta coping, and corner courtyard stair motifs were, however, dismantled and reconstructed in Oak Park at the entrance to a building of similar exterior design.

The large semicircular arch distinguishes the barrel-vaulted public entrance to the courtyard. The efflorescent terra-cotta ornament within the spandrels clearly reflects Wright's training with Louis Sullivan.

Frank Lloyd Wright Home and Studio

Begun 1889

951 Chicago Ave.
Oak Park, IL 60302
(312) 994-4000

flwright.org/visit/
homeandstudio

56

ILLINOIS

Frank Lloyd Wright was a twenty-two-year-old draftsman when he borrowed $5,000 from his employer, Louis Sullivan, to buy a corner lot and build a home for his family. The exterior of the house reflects an interest in the Shingle-style designs then popular on the East Coast. The building also exhibits features that foreshadow Wright's ultimate philosophy of architecture: the emphasis on pure geometric forms, the broad, sheltering roof, the use of natural materials, and the unity of building and site.

The living room fireplace hearth would be the center of family life. From it, the plan of the first floor develops outward, pinwheeling from the masonry core of the living room and dining room fireplaces. The interior space is remarkably open, lacking the characteristic Victorian hierarchy of reception rooms, formal parlors, and related spaces reserved for public use over private spaces for the family.

In 1895, Wright expanded the living space of the home by reconfiguring the original kitchen into a new dining room and adding on a new kitchen with a barrel-vaulted playroom above it. The dining room was Wright's first attempt at totally unifying the design of a room, from integrated lighting and mechanical systems to furnishings and decorative arts. The playroom, with its massive fireplace, mural, skylight, built-in

seating, and cabinetry, offered a stimulating yet practical space for the neighborhood kindergarten (directed by Wright's first wife) and doubled as a recital space for the musically inclined family.

In 1898, the young architect joined his professional and personal lives with the addition of a four-room studio on Chicago Avenue. Comprising a two-story, octagonal drafting room, reception hall, private office, and library, the studio was the birthplace of the first distinctly American style of design, the Prairie School. Wright employed fourteen apprentices and associates during his Oak Park tenure and completed the designs for at least 125 buildings, one quarter of his life's work.

The drafting room, a vertical space lit from above and encircled by a balcony, clearly established the form Wright adopted for many great public commissions to follow: Unity Temple, the Larkin Administration Building, the SC Johnson Administration Building, and the Guggenheim Museum. The home and studio served as a laboratory for Wright's ceaseless experimentation with light, space, and decorative forms.

In 1974, the Frank Lloyd Wright Home and Studio Foundation, now the Frank Lloyd Wright Trust, was established to acquire the building and restore it to its state in 1909, the year Wright left Oak Park.

■ Unity Temple

1905

875 Lake St.
Oak Park, IL 60301
(708) 383-8873

utrf.org

When Unity Church of Oak Park, a congregation of Unitarians and Universalists, was struck by lightning and burned in 1905, Frank Lloyd Wright was commissioned to design a new building for the congregation. He faced several challenges, including a modest budget of $45,000 and a small, narrow site on a noisy main street.

Wright's solutions, including the choice of reinforced concrete as the building material and the bold simplicity of the cubist design, were unprecedented. The material produced a monumental facade at minimal cost, afforded privacy, and muffled street noise. Ornament was cast into the form, eliminating the expense of a brick or plaster veneer. The flat slab concrete roof cantilevers over the side walls to shelter the entrances and walkways.

Wright produced thirty-four studies before finalizing the design for the temple. The plan answered the congregation's need for functionally distinct areas, with two large spaces—a square sanctuary on the north and a rectangular meeting house on the south—connected by a shared central entrance hall. Access to the building is through a raised terrace on either side. The low ceiling of the entrance hall contrasts dramatically with the two-story central space of the adjoining rooms. Low corridors leading from the entry hall along the sides of the sanctuary to the rear of the room allow latecomers to enter without disturbing the service. Exits, however, are placed on either side of the pulpit, directing the congregants toward the minister as they depart. Tiers of seats on three sides accommodate four hundred people, yet no congregant is seated more than forty-five feet from the pulpit. This remarkably intimate space is enriched by the geometric patterns of the wood trim and the art-glass skylights typical of Wright's Prairie designs.

Unity Temple has been in continuous use since 1908 by the same congregation (now Unitarian-Universalist). Tours are expected to resume in 2017, following a large-scale restoration.

Waller Gates

1901

Six rock-face, cut-limestone pylons—set on concrete base skirts and topped with dressed-stone caps—and two metal fence sections remain from what was once the impressive entrance gate Frank Lloyd Wright designed for Edward C. Waller. A wealthy businessman and one of Wright's earliest patrons, Waller owned a six-acre estate along the Des Plaines River. In 1889, he commissioned the young architect to remodel the dining room of his twenty-four-room mansion and to design a gardener's cottage and stable.

The gates, which have been partially restored with replicas of the original lanterns, were first constructed after Waller sold a portion of his land to William Winslow. In 1893 Wright designed a residence for Winslow that stands just inside the gateway at 515 Auvergne Place. The fence sections were almost certainly fabricated from rolled steel at William Winslow's ornamental ironworks. The original construction also included a double-drive gate over the roadway, two flanking walkway gates, and square gaslight lanterns with brass frames atop the center piers.

4646 Spring Brook Rd.
Rockford, IL 61114
(815) 877-2952

laurenthouse.com

Kenneth and Phyllis Laurent House

1949

The Laurent House has the distinction of being the only house Frank Lloyd Wright designed for a wheelchair-bound client. Kenneth Laurent developed a spinal cord tumor while serving in the navy in World War II; the surgery to remove it left him paralyzed from the waist down. Laurent wrote to Wright in the summer of 1948 requesting he design a house suited to his needs. "I am confined to a wheelchair," Laurent wrote. "This explains my need for a home as practical and sensible as your style of architecture denotes."

Completed in 1952, the Laurent House predated the Americans with Disabilities Act by nearly four decades. The open floor plan and efficient use of space that characterized Wright's Usonian houses are present, with much consideration given to customizations made to meet Laurent's needs. There are no thresholds to obstruct a wheelchair, and the floor is level with the walkways outside. Doorways, hallways, and bathrooms are wider than usual so that Laurent could turn his wheelchair around rather than back out of a space. Doorknobs, light switches, and built-in cabinets with fold-down doors were at a height accessible to Laurent. The Wright-designed furniture was also built lower than usual so guests sat at or below Laurent's eye level. The house, constructed with

Chicago common brick and red tidewater cypress, is only the second (and first to be a single story) designed using Wright's hemicycle form. Intersecting arc shapes define both the interior living area and the brick half wall that encloses an outdoor terrace. At the rear of the house, the wooded lot slopes down to a creek.

In 1958 the Laurents approached Wright to design an addition, but the architect died before it could be built. Wright apprentice John Howe later provided the working drawings and supervised the project, which increased the square footage from about 1,400 square feet to 2,600 square feet and added an additional bedroom wing in the space of the original carport. The Laurents were the sole residents of the house from 1952 to 2012, when the property and original Wright-designed furniture were acquired by the Laurent House Foundation. The nonprofit organization undertook renovations, including the installation of a new roof and restoration of the Cherokee-Red concrete floors that had been covered over with carpet. In June 2014, the Laurent House opened to the public as a house museum. Regular guided tours are available with a reservation.

301 E. Lawrence Ave.
Springfield, IL 62703
(217) 782-6776

dana-thomas.org

Dana-Thomas House ■

Susan Lawrence Dana House

1902–4

The thirty-five-room mansion Frank Lloyd Wright designed for Susan Lawrence Dana is the largest and most comprehensive example of the architect's Prairie-period houses to have survived. Dana, a wealthy widow and social activist, wanted a house suited to her social ambition and lavish style of entertaining. The project, which started as a remodeling of the Lawrence family's 1868 home, soon eclipsed the earlier dwelling. Wright's double cross-axis plan incorporated vestiges of the original building in the foundation, walls, and fireplace in accordance with Dana's wishes.

Unfettered by financial considerations, thirty-five-year-old Wright faced both an unprecedented opportunity and formidable challenge. The project commanded the resources of his studio and several collaborating artisans for two years. The result was an extraordinarily complex and sophisticated integration of architecture, furnishings, and decorative arts, a complete and unified statement of the Prairie school aesthetic.

The massive arched entrance is an appropriately dramatic introduction to the twelve-thousand-square-foot residence. The buff-colored brick of the exterior walls extends to an upper-level frieze of plaster

panels, framing the art-glass casement windows. The gable roof and unusual flaring copper gutters lend an Asian character to the building.

The principal public areas of the house—reception hall, dining room, and gallery—are centrally located on the raised first floor. These vast, open, double-height spaces—complete with musicians' balconies—were an ideal stage for concerts, lectures, and elaborate social gatherings. The lower level contained a billiard room, bowling alley, and library, among whose patrons were the neighborhood children.

Wright proved a brilliant manager of a project so large in scale. More than 450 pieces of art glass, including two hundred light fixtures, and more than one hundred pieces of oak furniture were designed and produced for the site. The exceptionally varied art-glass designs were inspired by butterflies and sumac plants. Richard Bock was responsible for the sculptures, and George M. Niedecken painted the dining room mural.

Dana remained in the house until 1928, after which the Thomas Publishing Company purchased the property in 1944. The site was acquired by the State of Illinois in 1981. A $5 million restoration was completed in 1990, with an additional $2.3 million in mechanical work done in 2011.

Lawrence Education Center
101 E. Laurel St.
Springfield, IL 62704
(217) 525-3144

www.sps186.org/schools/
lawrence/library

Lawrence Memorial
Library Reconstruction
1905

Susan Lawrence Dana's patronage of Frank Lloyd Wright extended beyond the design of her magnificent Springfield residence. As a memorial to her father, Rheuna Lawrence, president of the Springfield School Board at the time of his death in 1901, she commissioned Wright to design a small library for the west room of a 1903 elementary school. It's believed that the library was not open until 1910, when Dana's contribution was recognized in the local newspaper. Designed similar in plan to Dana's private library in her Springfield home, the commission was somewhat unusual, as it required Wright to design an interior space within an existing building. During the 1930s, the room was dismantled to provide additional classroom space and was virtually forgotten. In 1981, the Dana-Thomas House was acquired by the State of Illinois; during the process of a historic building survey, Wright's drawings for the library were rediscovered, dispelling assumptions that the Lawrence Library was part of Dana's residence.

The library was reconstructed in 1992 and furnished according to Wright's original design. A short, oak-spindled wall runs the length of the room, dividing the public reading area from the stacks. Four alcoves along the south wall are lined with bookshelves. The bookcases flanking the large east windows create recesses for window seats, and an L-shaped bench wraps the rear wall.

The library is open to visitors for regular hours during the school year and limited hours over the summer.

Samara

John and Catherine Christian House

1954

1301 Woodland Ave.
West Lafayette, IN 47906
(765) 409-5522

samara-house.org

66

INDIANA

Commonly known as Samara, after the winged seed motif that recurs throughout, the Christian House demonstrates Frank Lloyd Wright's Usonian vision of affordable houses capable of meeting the needs of a growing family. It was occupied by its original owner, Dr. John Christian, until 2015. The Christians worked closely with Wright on all details. Catherine Christian developed the program for the project, writing a twenty-seven-page typewritten essay, "What We Need for How We Live," for Wright's reference while planning their house. In it, she provided the architect with a short biography and portrait of each family member, a narrative on how they hoped to use the house for living as well as entertaining, and a room-by-room accounting of current and future estimates for furnishings, storage, and equipment needs. "We want a home and its surroundings to have a future," she wrote. "One that will grow with us."

Wright's studio went into full production mode in August 1953, with the final set of twenty drawings ultimately approved by the Christians in January 1955. The final plan includes a spacious sunken living room with three steps leading up to seats running along one side and three steps leading up to the dining area on the opposite side. The dining area opens

on two sides onto a lanai, which curves from the entrance driveway to also meet the master and guest bedrooms.

The Christians impressed upon their architect that their finances were limited and they would need to complete elements of Samara over time, something Wright understood and planned for in his design. The home was constructed so that decorative elements, such as the distinctive copper roof fascia and Philippine mahogany clerestory panels, could be completed after the family took possession of their home in September 1956.

Tours of Samara are available by reservation.

George and Eleanor Stockman House

530 1st St. N.E.
Mason City, IA 50401
(641) 423-1923

stockmanhouse.org

1908

Frank Lloyd Wright first published a variation on the plan of this compact Prairie-style house as "a Fireproof House for $5,000" in a 1907 issue of the *Ladies' Home Journal*. Dr. G. C. Stockman was a friend of J. E. E. Markley and James Blythe, who commissioned Wright to design the City National Bank and Park Inn Hotel in Mason City.

The nearly square first-floor plan of the Stockman House opens to a veranda on one side and a large entry hall with a cantilevered eave on the opposite side. The living room and dining room are essentially continuous, separated only by the fireplace block. The kitchen is at the rear, and the four bedrooms are all on the second floor. The house contains examples of Arts and Crafts and Wright-designed furnishings of the period.

The windows, in true Prairie fashion, are grouped in horizontal bands underscored by long window boxes. The projecting eaves extend the line of the low, hipped roof, conveying a sense of shelter. The continuous wood trim wrapping the corners of the main block, as well as the dark window frames, roof fascia, and base, delineate the simple but subtle geometry of Wright's composition.

The house was the only Wright-designed residence actually built in Mason City, although he designed at least one proposal for a house in

the Rock Crest subdivision. By 1917 this development contained eight dwellings designed by former associates and apprentices in Wright's Oak Park studio: Francis Barry Byrne, William Drummond, Walter Burley Griffin, and Marion Mahony Griffin. Several of the houses share the open floor plan, which, once published, was adopted by builders in many parts of the Midwest as an affordable, comfortable family home.

In 1989 the Stockman House was moved to its present location, adjacent to the Rock Crest/Rock Glen National Historic District, where it was restored by its current owner, the River City Society for Historic Preservation. The Robert E. McCoy Architectural Interpretive Center is located next door. Regular tours are offered seasonally, and tours may be scheduled by appointment in the off-season.

Historic Park Inn Hotel

Park Inn Hotel and City National Bank

1909

7 W. State St.
Mason City, IA 50401
(641) 422-0015

historicparkinn.com

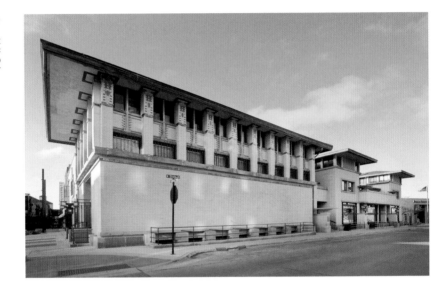

Frank Lloyd Wright described the bank he designed for this turn-of-the-century prairie boomtown as a "strong box on a large scale, a well-aired and lighted fireproof vault." The clients were lawyers in the firm Blythe, Markley, Rule and Smith.

This large commission included the design of two buildings: the bank and an adjoining hotel. The bank's imposing facade dominated the corner lot: a sixteen-foot-high solid masonry wall formed the exterior of the ground floor. Brick piers with colored terra-cotta ornament extended from a sandstone belt course to the roofline and framed the recessed art-glass windows. Parallel ranges of windows provided natural light for third-floor offices and the main banking room. Art-glass skylights lit the one-story extension on the south side of the bank, which contained the president's office and the boardroom.

The hotel was small, accommodating fewer than fifty guests. The dining room featured a large art-glass skylight, and the open porch on the second floor overlooked the town's central park. Offices for the law firm were located on the second floor of the hotel's east wing and on the top floor of the bank. The hotel's west wing contained ground-floor retail space.

Construction was under way in 1909 when Wright left for a Euro-pean sabbatical. The building opened in 1910, and the ground floor of the bank was converted to a retail space in 1926. Remodeling includ-ed the installation of large display windows, which compromised the impressive masonry exterior of Wright's design. In addition, a second floor of offices was located at the level of the former clerestory windows, which were enlarged, moving the horizontal belt course downward. Wright's design is faithfully represented by the upper-level ornamenta-tion and wood-muntin windows.

In 2011, after a two-year renovation that included significant resto-ration and reconstruction and returned the exterior to Wright's origi-nal design, the Historic Park Inn Hotel opened with twenty-seven guest rooms, a restaurant and bar, and an event space housed in the former bank building. Wright on the Park, Inc., the nonprofit organization that owns the hotel, offers regular docent-led tours of the structure.

Cedar Rock

Lowell and Agnes Walter House

1945

2611 Quasqueton Diagonal Blvd.
Quasqueton, IA 50644
(319) 934-3572
friendsofcedarrock.org

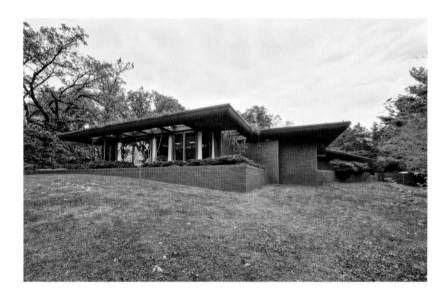

A limestone bluff high above a bend in Iowa's Wapsipinicon River provided a stunning site for a complex of buildings—dubbed Cedar Rock by Frank Lloyd Wright—that served as a summer retreat for Des Moines businessman Lowell Walter and his wife, Agnes. The eleven-acre site includes the main house, a two-story boathouse, an outdoor hearth, and an entrance gate. Walter commissioned the design in 1942, but wartime restrictions on materials delayed construction until 1948. In 1945, Frank Lloyd Wright published the design he referred to as a "glass house" in the *Ladies' Home Journal.*

The main living area of the Walter House is a nine-hundred-square-foot combined living room, dining alcove, and conservatory. Three exterior glass walls afford a spectacular view of the river and valley floor, while a central clerestory and skylights provide an interior garden with natural light. The plan extends from the main living area at an angle, in a wing containing the bedrooms, utility and storage areas, bathrooms, and carport.

The walnut board-and-batten interior walls, cabinetry, and furnishings were all executed according to Wright's specifications. The bathrooms are Pullman-type modules installed as a unit. The heated floor

mat is concrete, as is the roof, with its broad overhangs and curved perimeter designed to support rooftop plantings.

Upon Lowell's death in 1981, Cedar Rock was left to Agnes, who, in accordance with his will, donated the house to the people of Iowa in 1982. The Iowa Department of Natural Resources administers the house, offering guided tours seasonally.

Corbin Education Center

Juvenile Cultural Center

1958

Wichita State University
1845 Fairmount St.
Wichita, KS 67260

http://bit.ly/2cshbaZ

Frank Lloyd Wright was commissioned in 1957 to design classroom, office, and laboratory space for Wichita State University's College of Education. Wright's preliminary plans were completed in 1958, but inadequate funding delayed construction until 1963, when only one of two designed buildings was completed.

The concrete and steel structure is supported by two hundred pylons sunk into a bed of clay. An esplanade with a fountain and reflecting pool separates the center's two two-story wings. The building contains more than twenty-seven thousand square feet with an additional thirteen thousand square feet of sheltered outdoor balconies and terraces. The interior floor is red vinyl tile, and trim, cabinetry, and custom furniture are made from solid, clear red oak. The exterior red brick was laid with matching mortar and raked horizontal joints. The fenestration includes large exposures of polished plate glass, which were later covered with bronze screen sunshades. The roof fascia is exposed stone aggregate, colored to blend with the brick. The concrete canopies of the belvederes are rimmed with turquoise fascia. Slender light towers extend sixty feet through openings in the canopies.

The center is open to visitors when university classes are in session.

Henry and Elsie Allen House

1915

255 N. Roosevelt St.
Wichita, ᴋѕ 67208
(316) 687-1027

flwrightwichita.org

Henry and Elsie Allen commissioned Frank Lloyd Wright to design a home for their corner lot in College Hill, then a newly developed residential neighborhood of east Wichita. Wright delivered the initial design in late December 1915. In 1918 the Allens moved in, and from 1919 to 1923, Henry Allen served as governor of Kansas.

The Allen House is among the last of Wright's Prairie residences. It at once recalls the early Prairie houses and prefigures the Usonians of the 1930s. Wright designed the Allen House while working on plans for the Imperial Hotel in Tokyo, and this Japanese influence is visible in the red clay tile roof and the enclosed garden, with its lily pool and garden house reminiscent of a Japanese teahouse.

The residence is L-shaped. The one-story wing at the front of the lot contains the entrance hall and 945-square-foot living room with a massive fireplace and bookshelf-lined alcove. The two-story wing to the south comprises the first-floor dining room with an art-glass ceiling, kitchen, servant's quarters, and two-car garage at ground level. On the second floor are Governor Allen's library, Mrs. Allen's study, bedrooms, and a guest suite. The interiors are exceptionally rich, with art glass in windows and bookcase doors, as well as gilding applied to the horizontal

joints of the masonry walls (a feature used elsewhere only at the Darwin D. Martin House and the Imperial Hotel in Tokyo). Brick scored with thin vertical lines is the dominant material inside and out. The wood trim is red gum, and the window sashes are cypress. Walnut furniture designed by Wright in collaboration with George M. Niedecken, who built the furniture for a number of Prairie houses in the Midwest, is displayed throughout the house.

The Allens lived in the house until 1949. In 1989 then-owner Arthur Kincade died and willed the house to the Wichita State University Endowment Association. The Allen House Foundation acquired the house in 1990 and has undertaken its restoration. Regular guided tours are offered with reservations.

Gregor and Elizabeth Affleck House

40925 N. Woodward Ave.
Bloomfield Hills, MI 48304

ltu.edu/affleck_house

1940

The design of this 2,350-square-foot house demonstrates the adaptation of Frank Lloyd Wright's Usonian plan to a steep site. The Affleck House is one of three Usonian dwellings constructed in Michigan between 1939 and 1941. Gregor Affleck had grown up in Spring Green, Wisconsin, and was acquainted with Wright's work and his mother's family. The residence cost approximately $19,000 to build in 1941, with an additional $7,000 going toward original furniture.

The plan is T-shaped, with the entrance at the crossing. Access to the main living area is through a skylit loggia with an open well to a lower-level garden and stream. The functions of living, dining, and work rooms are consolidated in a unified space that spans a forty-foot ravine. A balcony wraps two sides of the cantilevered living room. The bedroom wing, which contains three bedrooms and terminates in a ground-level master suite, anchors the house to the hill. At the center of the house an atrium with planter boxes looks down on a reflecting pool, and a window pulls up air cooled by the pool into the house for natural air conditioning. Exterior walls made from cypress shiplap siding are used instead of the board-and-batten style more typical of Wright's Usonian houses. The precision evident in the chamfered, overlapped boards and

mitered corners attests to the skill of Harold Turner, a general contractor responsible for the construction of a number of Usonian houses.

The Afflecks' children donated the house to Lawrence Technological University in 1978. The university has undertaken the restoration of the building, which has included correcting structural problems, reconstructing deteriorated sections, improving energy efficiency, and restoring the original appearance of the house. Over the years, it has been used as a teaching resource for the College of Architecture and Design.

Tours are offered on a seasonal, monthly basis.

Melvyn and Sara Smith House

1946

Tours offered through Cranbrook
Center for Collections and Research
39221 Woodward Ave.
Bloomfield Hills, MI 48303
(248) 645-3307

cranbrook.edu/center

Melvyn and Sara Smith were both schoolteachers in the Detroit school system with modest incomes. Melvyn Smith was determined to live in a house designed by Frank Lloyd Wright from the moment he saw a slide of Fallingwater as a young student.

Completed in 1950, the 1,800-square-foot Usonian is tucked into a small hill on wooded land in a suburb of Detroit. Its elongated, L-shaped plan is laid out on a two-by-four-foot grid. In one wing are three bedrooms; in the other, the dining and living area with a built-in lounge and shelving running the length of the wall. Characteristic of many Usonian designs, it has a simple facade, with brick and red tidewater cypress board-and-batten walls topped by a band of clerestory windows and wide, horizontal roof planes with large overhangs. In the rear, floor-to-ceiling windows open to a gently sloping hill, pond, and marshes. The landscaping was designed in the late 1950s by Thomas Church.

The house is now owned by a private foundation, which completed a meticulous restoration of the house in 2011, taking care to leave the furnishings and art collection of the original owners intact. The Cranbrook Center for Collections and Research conducts regular guided tours in the spring through fall that depart from the Cranbrook campus.

450 Madison Ave. S.E.
Grand Rapids, MI 49503
(616) 246-4821

meyermayhouse.steelcase.com

Meyer and Sophie May House
1908

Meyer May, a successful Grand Rapids clothier, and his wife, Sophie, commissioned Frank Lloyd Wright to design their family home in this western Michigan manufacturing town. Its horizontal emphasis, concrete water table, raked horizontal mortar joints, deep eaves, and rhythmic window groupings are hallmarks of Wright's mature Prairie houses. Although the May House is more compact in scale, the lean masonry masses, concrete-capped walls, and projecting roofline recall Wright's design of the Robie House, under construction during the same year.

The May House is pushed back to the north lot line, providing maximum space for the garden and optimum exposure for the art-glass windows and doors of the south facade. The entrance is at the rear of the dwelling. Narrow stairs lead to the main living area, where built-in cabinetry and screens fashioned of oak spindles in an open geometric pattern replace conventional walls as a means to define the interior space. The geometric oak trim throughout the house was scaled to the modest height of the owner.

Wright specified the use of reflective gold glass in the mortar joints of the fireplaces, where its iridescent sparkle lightens the dense masonry wall. In form and color, the design of the numerous art-glass windows,

framed ceiling panels over recessed lights, and lanterns of the dining room table draws its inspiration from abstracted plant forms. George M. Niedecken, an interior designer and Wright collaborator, was responsible for the execution of the furnishings and decorative arts throughout the house, including the hollyhock mural dividing the gallery and dining room.

In 1987 the house was purchased and restored by Steelcase, the Grand Rapids–based furniture company that built the Wright-designed office furniture for the SC Johnson Administration Building.

202 Cloquet Ave.
Cloquet, MN 55720

Lindholm Oil Company Service Station

1956

■

In 1932, Frank Lloyd Wright designed his Standardized Service Station, a model for a prefabricated gas station that would be a component of his Broadacre City concept—a new urban landscape of thoughtfully designed houses, commercial and industrial buildings, parkland, agriculture, and automobile infrastructure.

The Lindholm Oil Company Service Station, in Cloquet, Minnesota, designed by Wright in 1956, is a variation of that prototype. Wright, well known to be an avid automobile enthusiast, hoped to eliminate the frequent "eyesores" lining American highways and to develop a facility that would offer a variety of customer services in addition to the sale of fuel.

When opened in 1958, the site attracted notice from far beyond this small northern Minnesota town, resulting in record pump sales for Phillips 66. Unique features of the steel and concrete building include a sixty-foot illuminated rooftop pylon, an upper-level glass observation lounge, and a cantilevered copper canopy. Wright designed the canopy to hold overhead hoses, thus eliminating the obstruction of pump islands. That scheme was abandoned because local fire codes required underground fuel storage. Ceramic tile walls, cypress trim, decorative planters, and skylights in the service bays were amenities that served to elevate the status of the humble filling station.

Although this is the only Wright-designed service station ever built, the arrangement of service bays around a central office, the V-shaped canopy, and the large canted windows were elements incorporated into a number of Phillips stations.

Francis and Mary Little House II Hallway Reconstruction

1912

Minneapolis Institute of Art
2400 Third Ave. S.
Minneapolis, MN 55404
(612) 870-3000

artsmia.org

In 1972, before being demolished, Francis and Mary Little's summer house in Deephaven, Minnesota, designed by Frank Lloyd Wright, was dismantled and sections were preserved by the Metropolitan Museum of Art in New York for exhibition. (For more on the Little House II, see p. 96 for the entry on the living room reconstruction.) Later that same year, the Minneapolis Institute of Art acquired the hallway that led to the master bedroom of the house.

The long and low Prairie-style house featured windows that spanned the entire facade overlooking Lake Minnetonka. Wright drew elaborate designs for these windows, but Francis Little did not want an intricate pattern to conceal the scenic lake view. They compromised with borders that frame an expanse of open glass. The border design becomes increasingly elaborate toward the right end of this hallway, which originally overlooked a grove of trees.

The hallway was installed in the museum without its fourth wall, which was made up of closets. The reconstruction is accessible during regular museum hours, and a model of the Little House II is also on display.

255 Bedford St. S.E.
Minneapolis, MN 55414

thewilleyhouse.com

Malcolm and Nancy Willey House

1933

Frank Lloyd Wright designed this Usonian house for Malcolm Willey, an administrator at the University of Minnesota, and his wife, Nancy, who, after reading Wright's autobiography, wrote the architect to request he design them a small house. With the American economy in ruins, the commission came at a time when Wright and his cadre of apprentices were in need of work. The Willeys would become the prototype for Wright's post-Depression clients. As Wright scholar Neil Levine described, they were a "more varied type from the upper-middle-class and wealthy group of businessmen and women who generally hired Wright in the years prior to the crash." With this house, Wright learned how to design for the middle class.

Wright's initial design for the house was two stories and twice the Willeys' budget. The scaled-down final plan built in 1934 is a one-story structure with a solid brick wall (penetrated only by small slit windows) facing the only neighboring house and floor-to-ceiling glass windows opening onto a terrace on the garden side. The living and dining areas share one space, highlighted by a massive chimney and large fireplace. Predating contemporary open-plan kitchens, the kitchen workspace uses shelving and glass to connect it more continuously to the living area

than in previous Wright designs. Built-in bookcases line the long, narrow hallway to the bedroom wing. In 2002 the house was acquired by its current owners, who undertook a five-and-a-half-year restoration.

The Willey House remains privately owned and is not open to the public on a daily basis, but occasional open houses are scheduled and group tours are available by prior arrangement with the owners.

509 E. Beach Dr.
Ocean Springs, MS 39564
(228) 523-4150
rhonda.price@dmr.ms.gov

msgulfcoastheritage.ms.gov

Charnley-Norwood House ■

James and Helen Charnley
Summer Cottage

1890

In the spring of 1890, while Frank Lloyd Wright was chief draftsman at Louis Sullivan's office, the firm designed this vacation house for James Charnley. A precursor to the Chicago residence Sullivan and Wright designed for Charnley the following year (now the Charnley-Persky House, see p. 42), the T-shaped main house and smaller octagonal guest cottage of the country residence sat directly on the Mississippi Gulf Coast and next to a similar house Sullivan designed and built for himself. The main house burned down in 1897 but was immediately rebuilt by Sullivan for Chicago businessman Frederick Norwood on the original site following the original plan.

In 2005, both the main house and the guest cottage were severely damaged by Hurricane Katrina. Fortunately, the Mississippi Department of Archives and History (MDAH), the National Trust for Historic Preservation, and the Frank Lloyd Wright Building Conservancy prevented their demolition, and the MDAH and Mississippi Department of Marine Resources funded a $2.3 million acquisition and restoration of the main house to its circa-1900 appearance. In 2013, the restored building, now owned by the State of Mississippi, opened to the public for tours by appointment.

Community
Christian Church

4601 Main St.
Kansas City, MO, 64112
(816) 561-6531

community-christian.org

1940

The building Frank Lloyd Wright planned for the congregation of Dr. Bur-ris A. Jenkins was to be what Wright called "the church of the future," but financial considerations, wartime shortages of materials, and restrictive building codes greatly compromised his original design. Forced to abandon the planned parking terraces, rooftop garden, and rock-ballast foundation, Wright lamented that the building was his only in shape.

The angular facade and plan conform to the irregularities of the sloping site. Wright employed a rhombus with two 120-degree angles and two 60-degree angles as the basic unit in the design. Gunite—an inexpensive, strong, fireproof, and lightweight concrete—was sprayed over sheets of corrugated steel that were then sandwiched together to form the walls. The innovative material allowed Wright to reduce the thickness of the walls to a mere 2¾ inches. When joined at wide angles, the walls thus have the appearance of folded planes. The main stairwell and chancel are hexagonal.

A perforated dome was constructed on the roof of the chancel, but the four searchlights necessary to illuminate the "Steeple of Light" Wright envisioned were not installed until 1994. (Dale Eldred, an internationally known light sculptor, was commissioned to complete the

lighting plan.) On weekends and holidays, the powerful lights project through the dome and reach up into the night sky. Exceptional acoustics and seating for nine hundred make the sanctuary a suitable space for musical performances as well as religious services. The small chapel, fellowship hall, and entrance from Main Street were later additions not of Wright's design.

The building is open for self-guided tours during office hours and guided tours by appointment.

The Frank Lloyd Wright
House in Ebsworth Park

Russell and Ruth Kraus House

1950

120 N. Ballas Rd.
Kirkwood, MO 63122
(314) 822-8359

ebsworthpark.org

Of the five Frank Lloyd Wright–designed buildings in Missouri, the house built for Russell and Ruth Kraus in Kirkwood, a suburb of St. Louis, is the only residential site open to the public. Construction began in 1951 and was completed in 1955. The Usonian house is situated in the center of a 10½-acre tract of woods and rolling meadows and is surrounded by a grove of tall, slender persimmon trees.

Known for its complex geometry, dominated by 60- and 120-degree parallelogram forms, the Kraus House consists of two overlapping parallelograms. The parallelogram is carried through to every detail of the house. Even the beds conform to the house's underlying shape. The interior and exterior of the house are executed in tidewater red cypress, brick, and concrete. Maple wood is used for counters in the workspace and birch wood for the cabinets.

One enters from the carport into a low-ceilinged corridor that runs the full length of the building. The expansive central living-and-dining area opens off the corridor with a workspace adjacent. At the north end of the house are two small bedrooms, a master bedroom, and a study. An artist's studio with a skylight is at the opposite end. A series of doors lead out onto a large, west-facing terrace, which is shaped

like the prow of a ship. Russell Kraus, a stained-glass artist by profession, added stained glass to the doors consistent with the geometry of the house. All of the original Wright-designed furnishings have been retained.

In January 2001, the Frank Lloyd Wright House in Ebsworth Park purchased the house and grounds to ensure their preservation and restoration. The nonprofit organization restored the house, built a road and parking area, and in 2011 added a Cherokee Red entrance gate originally designed by Wright for the Kraus House.

Guided tours of the house are available by appointment.

Isadore and Lucille Zimmerman House

1950

tours depart from:
Currier Museum of Art
150 Ash St.
Manchester, NH 03104
(603) 669-6144

currier.org/collections/
zimmerman-house

In their first letter to Frank Lloyd Wright, the Zimmermans described their "housing problem in ultra-conservative New England." Dissatisfied with the notion of building a traditional New Hampshire house, they wrote: "We wish to avoid adding a new antique to the city's architecture." Wright accepted the commission, designing what he called a classic Usonian.

The brick, cast-concrete, and cypress dwelling is sited diagonally on a ¾-acre lot. A high, continuous band of windows set in sand-colored concrete blocks relieves the solid masonry of the street facade. The garden facade, by contrast, is composed of floor-to-ceiling glass mitered at the corners.

Wright designed the landscape as well as all of the freestanding and built-in furniture. He also selected the textiles and the family's dinnerware. The use of built-ins, a continuous concrete floor mat, and dramatic changes in ceiling height make this small house seem larger than its 1,667 square feet.

In 1988 the building was bequeathed to the Currier Museum of Art, which undertook its restoration and now offers regular guided tours departing from the museum. Reservations are required.

125 Jewett Pkwy.
Buffalo, NY 14214
(716) 856-3858

darwinmartinhouse.org

Martin House Complex

Darwin D. Martin House

1903–5, 1909

The Darwin D. Martin House is admired for its six signature buildings, interior and exterior gardens, and an extraordinary collection of art glass and furnishings, all designed by Frank Lloyd Wright. The property is located in the planned community of Parkside, a historic neighborhood conceived by Frederick Law Olmsted Sr.

Darwin D. Martin was a remarkable client. An accomplished business and civic leader, he invited Wright to Buffalo to discuss a proposal for the design of an administrative headquarters for the Larkin Company, a burgeoning soap-manufacturing and mail-order conglomerate for which Martin served as chief executive officer. He also sought a new home for his wife, Isabelle, and their family commensurate with their rising social standing. Both commissions, facilitated by Martin, are regarded as the two most important of the architect's early career.

The elaborate multibuilding estate is defined by the union of three houses: the main Darwin D. Martin House (1904–5); the George and Delta Barton House (1903), constructed for Martin's sister Delta; and the Gardener's Cottage (1909). The property also contains a series of connecting buildings, including a pergola, conservatory, and carriage house, all of which were demolished in 1962 and reconstructed from

2006 to 2008 as part of a comprehensive restoration using Wright's original drawings.

The Barton House was the first dwelling to be built on the estate and set an important style precedent for the 1½-acre site; the modest house gave Wright the opportunity to display his artistic vision in anticipation of the principal structure. The Darwin D. Martin House is a quintessential expression of Wright's Prairie-house ideal, characterized by its low profile, cruciform plan, spatial openness, pronounced horizontality, dramatic pier-and-cantilever construction, and natural palette of materials. The completely integrated composition is distinguished for its elegant detailing, as exemplified by a wisteria-patterned glass mosaic adorning a focal fireplace in the home's entry hall. It is also made evident in the nearly four hundred individual art-glass windows throughout the estate. Additionally, there are numerous displays of fine wood craftsmanship in the form of custom moldings and built-in and freestanding furniture.

The grounds of the Martin House contain some of the most comprehensive residential gardens ever designed and executed by Wright. Of particular significance is the "floricycle," a blooming arc of colorful seasonal plantings that creates a soft, natural screen between the home and the surrounding streetscape. Walter Burley Griffin served as landscape architect.

The historic property has concluded an ambitious twenty-five-year restoration effort, the result of a strategic partnership between the nonprofit Martin House Restoration Corporation and the State of New York. A contemporary glass pavilion designed by Toshiko Mori opened in 2009 to function as the museum's primary visitor and interpretation center.

Graycliff ■

Isabelle Martin House

1926

Graycliff, the summer estate of Isabelle R. and Darwin D. Martin, is located fourteen miles southwest of Buffalo, New York, where Frank Lloyd Wright built the couple's full-time residence. One of the most extensive summer houses designed by the architect, the complex sits on an 8½-acre tract of land on a sixty-foot-high cliff above Lake Erie.

Wright created a 2½-acre compound on the site organized around a circular drive. He planned for a main house, guest house, chauffeur's house and garage, caretakers' cottage, and boiler house. Extensive landscape features included three sunken gardens, stone walls, a tennis court, and a pier extending into the lake. Of the proposed buildings, only three were built. The main house and chauffeur's house form an L shape and are connected by a garden wall. The third building—the boiler house—is partially recessed into the courtyard between the main and secondary houses. All of these structures were built between 1926 and 1931. The stock market crash of 1929 caused the Martins to become more conservative with their spending, and a less elaborate landscape plan by landscape architect Ellen Biddle Shipman, created that year, was partially implemented. These alterations removed some features of the original Wright-designed landscape. The chauffeur's house was expanded by Wright and then adapted for use by the Martins' daughter, Dorothy Martin Foster, and her family, with living spaces on the second story, above a four-vehicle garage and service spaces.

The main house comprises two buildings joined by a second-story bridge measuring forty-six feet wide. On clear days, the spray of Niagara Falls is visible through the opening framed by the bridge and two buildings. Second-floor balconies serve as viewing platforms offering vistas of the lake and, in the distance, the city of Buffalo.

The estate was purchased in 1999 by the Graycliff Conservancy, a nonprofit organization whose mission is to return the complex to its 1930 appearance. Exterior restoration has been completed, and interior restoration continues without the interruption of tours.

Francis and Mary Little House II Living Room Reconstruction

1912

Metropolitan Museum of Art
1000 Fifth Ave.
New York, NY 10028
(212) 535-7710

metmuseum.org

Frank Lloyd Wright's Midwestern Prairie house for the Little family stretched 250 feet along the wooded shore of Lake Minnetonka in Deephaven, Minnesota. When all attempts by the Littles to find a suitable buyer or alternate use for the house failed in the early 1970s, the house was slated for demolition. At that point, the Metropolitan Museum of Art stepped in to save parts of the structure before it was razed in 1972. The Little House library was installed in the Allentown Art Museum in Pennsylvania (see p. 107), and its hallway is at the Minneapolis Institute of Art (see p. 84). The fifty-five-foot-long pavilion containing the living room, on display at the Metropolitan Museum of Art, originally crowned a knoll and functioned as a space for musical recitals and for entertaining. The house had two entrances: one led to a vestibule opening into the living room, while a separate door farther down the terrace led to the family's quarters. A small interior opening connected the two main areas of the house.

Twelve paired art-glass panels were centered along each of the side walls. The pattern of clear and opaque white glass created a kind of decorative border framing views of the lake and the surrounding woods. The art-glass design was repeated in the clerestory windows and in the five laylights that were illuminated at night by electric lamps.

The simplicity and minimal color of the final design pleased Little, who wanted no impediment to the lake view nor to the amount of natural light entering the room. Narrow bands of white oak trimmed the wall surfaces, framed the window and laylight openings, and extended across the coved ceiling.

The reconstructed room's furnishings are original Wright designs, although some were for the Littles' first house, designed by Wright in 1903, in Peoria, Illinois. Among the earlier pieces are the print table, the plant stands, the armchairs, and the reading table. The other furnishings, including six standing lamps, a library table, end table, and light fixtures, were executed as a group for this later house.

1071 Fifth Ave.
New York, NY 10128
(212) 423-3500

guggenheim.org

Solomon R. Guggenheim Museum

1943

■

Few buildings have inspired the level of controversy generated by Frank Lloyd Wright's highly unconventional design of the Guggenheim Museum. Solomon R. Guggenheim commissioned the museum in 1943, but thirteen years passed before ground was broken. The design and construction of the museum required more than seven hundred drawings and an additional six sets of construction documents. Wright waged exhaustive battles with New York City officials, whose outdated building codes had no relevance to his design. The museum opened shortly after Wright's death in 1959.

Wright's plan provided for several spaces: the main gallery; an adjoining, smaller circular structure—the monitor building, as Wright called it—for administrative offices; and an annex, which was completed in a modified form in 1968 by Wright's associate William Wesley Peters. Wright called the gradually opening, cast-concrete form a ziggurat. The design is purely sculptural, free of surface embellishments. The curving, streamlined exterior establishes a pattern of wall and void that corresponds to changes in level on the interior. Inside the main gallery, a quarter-mile-long, cantilevered ramp curves continuously as it rises seventy-five feet to the roof. A twelve-sided, web-patterned domed skylight covers the building and floods the interior with natural light. Works of art are displayed on the ground floor and in the seventy-four circular bays that line the walls of the ramp. A lower-level auditorium accommodates three hundred people.

In 1989, construction began on a ten-story tower to provide an additional thirty-one thousand square feet of exhibition space at the rear of the building. The expansion program also added a ten-thousand-square-foot under-ground vault for administrative offices. In 1990, the museum closed for restoration, reopening in 1992 with state-of-the-art climate control and security systems, new roofs, laminated, light-filtering glass in the skylights, a new cafe, and an expanded store. The monitor building, renamed the Thannhauser Build-ing, was converted into an exhibition space. In 2008 another multiyear restoration was completed, during which eleven coats of exterior paint were removed.

534 Morgan St.
Oberlin, OH 44074
(440) 775-8671

oberlin.edu/amam/
flwright.html

Weltzheimer-Johnson House

Charles and Margaret Weltzheimer House

1947

The Usonian house was an efficient, comfortable, and attractive dwelling that Frank Lloyd Wright intended to match the needs and limited budget of the modern middle-American family. The Weltzheimers, a family of six with a construction budget of $15,000, were ideal candidates. However, the completed house cost in excess of $50,000 in 1950, due in part to the relatively large scale of the dwelling, numerous changes made during construction, and extensive use of masonry and decorative millwork.

The siting of the house, well back and at a forty-five-degree angle on a long, narrow lot, affords maximum use and views of the property. The single-story, flat-roofed, L-shaped plan has combined living and dining areas set at a right angle to the bedroom wing—all consistent with earlier Usonian designs.

Other typical Usonian features include the use of built-in furnishings, cabinetry, and lighting to enhance the sense of interior spaciousness and preserve a unified style throughout the house. The clerestory windows and a largely glass wall on the southern end of the house minimize the distinction between the interior and exterior. The hemispherical ornament of the fascia and curvilinear cutouts in the clerestory panels are unique to the design of this house.

Margaret Weltzheimer lived in the house until her death in 1963. Two subsequent owners made significant alterations, but in 1968 Ellen H. Johnson, an art history professor, purchased the house and undertook its restoration. She lived there until her death in 1992. The site is now owned and administered by Oberlin College, which holds a monthly open house on a seasonal basis.

Burton and Orpha Westcott House

1906

The only house in Ohio designed by Frank Lloyd Wright in the Prairie style belonged to prominent businessman and city councilman Burton Westcott and his wife, Orpha. Built in 1907, the Westcott House shows the strong influence of Wright's 1905 trip to Japan.

The house is cruciform in plan. A fireplace surrounded by two ingle-nooks, complete with built-in benches, occupies its center and opens onto the living area. The main entryway and staircase are illuminated by a clerestory and skylight filled with art glass. The second-story spaces contained bedrooms for the Westcotts and their two children, and two servants' quarters. A ninety-foot pergola joins the main house to the carriage house. One of the longest designed by Wright, it makes an asset of the long, narrow site. The original garage stored cars produced by the Westcott Motor Car Company, which was founded by Mr. Westcott in 1909. Wright also designed small pony stalls as part of the structure.

After Mr. Westcott's death in 1926, the house was subdivided into a multiunit apartment building in the early 1940s, destroying the architectural integrity of Wright's design. Its condition severely deteriorated over the years. By 1996, the Frank Lloyd Wright Building Conservancy began a years-long intervention to save the house, purchasing it from the then

owner and completing urgent stabilization work before selling it to the Westcott House Foundation for full restoration in 2001. The restoration and furnishing of the house was completed in 2005, when it was opened to the public as a historic house museum.

510 Dewey Ave.
Bartlesville, OK 74003
(918) 336-4949

pricetower.org

Price Tower

1952

When Harold C. Price approached Frank Lloyd Wright with the prospect of designing a building for his pipeline construction firm, he envisioned a two- or three-story structure with parking for ten trucks. Wright rejected the concept as inefficient. Several months later, he presented Price with drawings for a nineteen-story, thirty-seven-thousand-square-foot, multiuse tower that would serve as corporate headquarters for the company, with additional space for apartments and professional offices. Construction began in late 1953 and was completed in 1956. The client and architect enjoyed an easy relationship; Wright designed two houses for members of the Price family, one in Bartlesville in 1953 and one in Arizona in 1954.

The precedent for what Wright called the "tree that escaped the crowded forest" was an unexecuted 1925 design for a New York City apartment building, St. Mark's Tower. Wright described the design as a treelike mast; its concrete floor slabs cantilever like branches from four interior vertical supports of steel-reinforced concrete. Freed of their load-bearing function, the exterior walls become ornamental screens. The angled faces of the tower were constructed from twenty-inch copper louvers that shade the window surfaces, sheets of stamped copper, and gold-tinted glass.

The upper floors of the Price Tower are divided into quadrants, one for two-story apartments and the other three for offices. The H. C. Price Company corporate apartment, on the seventeenth and eighteenth floors, features Wright-designed furniture and textiles and a Wright-designed mural entitled *The Blue Moon*. Harold Price Sr.'s office, located a story above in the penthouse, featured Wright-designed furniture, a functioning fireplace, three terraces, and a glass mural designed by Eugene Masselink. These three floors have been restored to their 1956 appearance and are open for regular tours.

In 1981, Phillips Petroleum purchased the building and opened the Bartlesville Museum on the first two floors. The museum was later reorganized in 1998 as the Price Tower Arts Center, which in 2001 took ownership of the building when Phillips Petroleum donated it to the nonprofit organization. Architect Wendy Evans Joseph remodeled eight floors of the tower into the Inn at Price Tower, a nineteen-room hotel, and the fifteenth-floor Copper Restaurant and Bar, which opened in 2003.

Conrad and Evelyn Gordon House
1956

■

In 1938, *LIFE* magazine commissioned Frank Lloyd Wright to design a house affordable to a family with an annual income of $5,000 to $6,000. The Gordon House is one of only two houses built according to that scheme. Commissioned by Conrad and Evelyn Gordon of Wilsonville, Oregon, the house was completed in 1963—four years after Wright's death—by Wright apprentice Burton Goodrich. (The other house built according to the 1938 scheme is Still Bend, built for Bernard and Fern Schwartz in Two Rivers, Wisconsin, completed in 1939.)

Although intended for clients living on a modest income, the Gordon House has a feeling of grandeur. Usonian in design, the house is planned on a seven-foot-square module—the largest module used in any of Wright's residential commissions. The great room, containing living, library, and dining areas, is a story and a half tall. Full-height doors open onto terraces that looked east toward Mt. Hood and west toward the Willamette River. Bands of narrow windows enclosed by perforated plywood boards admit light into the room in an abstract pattern. Such organic, passive-energy controls are classic Wright concepts.

Evelyn Gordon lived in the house until 1997. In late 2000, the Frank Lloyd Wright Building Conservancy and AIA Oregon convinced the new owners of the property to donate, rather than destroy, the structure. The house was dismantled and moved twenty-eight miles south to the Oregon Garden in Silverton, where it was reconstructed on a new concrete slab. The Gordon House is the only realized building designed by Wright in Oregon and the only Wright building in the Pacific Northwest open to the public. The Gordon House Conservancy oversees the ongoing restoration and operation of the house as a historic site and museum that has been open to the public since 2002.

Donald and Elizabeth Duncan House

1956

Polymath Park
187 Evergreen Ln.
Acme, PA 15610
(877) 833-7829

franklloydwrightovernight.net

Frank Lloyd Wright maintained an interest in prefabricated housing that continued into his late years. In 1956 he designed the first of three prefabricated housing models for Marshall Erdman, his contractor on the Unitarian Meeting House (see p. 120) in Madison, Wisconsin. Similar to the American System-Built Houses of 1915 (see p. 122), buyers would receive a set of all the major pieces they needed to assemble the house.

Originally constructed in 1957 in the Chicago suburb of Lisle, Illinois, the Duncan House is one of nine houses that were built on the Erdman Homes Prefab #1 plan. Others were constructed in Wisconsin, Minnesota, and New York. (Prefab #2 was a two-story plan and two were built; no Prefab #3 models were built.) It has a single-story, elongated L-shaped plan with three bedrooms, a carport, and a basement. The living space directly off the entrance is sunken by three steps and has vaulted ceilings. The exterior siding is textured Masonite board with horizontal battens. Concrete block was used for the original masonry core.

When Donald Duncan died in 2002, a developer acquired the property and planned to build several houses on the acreage. Demolition of the house was a certainty unless it could be moved. The Frank Lloyd Wright Building Conservancy facilitated the transfer of the house to Pennsylvania, where in 2007 it was rebuilt at the 130-acre Polymath Park. Sandstone was used to replace the concrete-block masonry of the original construction.

Polymath Park offers regular tours and overnight stays at the Duncan House as well as at two houses designed by Wright apprentice Peter Berndtson. In 2016, the owners acquired the R. W. Lindholm House—designed by Wright in 1952 and built in Cloquet, Minnesota—after it was threatened by encroaching retail development in its original location. That Usonian house will be reconstructed at Polymath Park and eventually opened to the public.

31 N. Fifth St.
Allentown, PA 18101
(610) 432-4333

allentownartmuseum.org

Francis and Mary Little House II Library Reconstruction

1912

The large and complex house Frank Lloyd Wright designed for Francis and Mary Little on Minnesota's Lake Minnetonka was among the richest expressions of the Prairie aesthetic. Before the building was demolished in 1972, critical sections were saved, including this library.

Originally located to the left of the house's asymmetrically placed entrance, the library functioned primarily as a reception area. Large art-glass windows on the east and south walls overlooked a terrace and the lawn respectively. The west wall was lined with oak bookshelves.

When the library was reconstructed in the Allentown Art Museum as part of a 1975 expansion, the architect, Edgar Tafel, followed a scheme used elsewhere in the house and added concealed lighting and parallel bands of oak trim to the ceiling. The furnishings are not original but are consistent with Wright's style of interior design: the barrel chairs are reproductions of those he designed for several other houses, the Wright-designed wall sconces in the Littles' living room were reproduced for this installation, and decorative objects from the museum's collection reflect Wright's aesthetic, including Chinese porcelain ginger jars, Japanese *ukiyo-e* prints, and a Gustav Stickley plant stand.

The library is one of three intact spaces from the Littles' Minnesota property on exhibit. The reconstructed living room is on display at the Metropolitan Museum of Art in New York (see p. 96) and a hallway at the Minneapolis Institute of Art (see p. 84).

Kentuck Knob

I. N. and Bernardine Hagan House

1954

723 Kentuck Rd.
Chalk Hill, PA 15421
(724) 329-1901

kentuckknob.com

Kentuck Knob is a Usonian single-family house based on a typical modular system; in this case, the module is an equilateral triangle measuring four-feet-six-inches per side. Unlike earlier Usonians, this house is highly customized. At the clients' request, Frank Lloyd Wright increased the size of the living and dining areas and carefully crafted the house in native stone, tidewater cypress, and copper. As at nearby Fallingwater, he laid a flagstone floor and set the walls with irregularly sized stones to create a more natural appearance.

Kentuck Knob's similarities to Fallingwater were deliberate. I. N. Hagan operated a dairy business in Uniontown, southwest of Fallingwater. He was approached by department store owner Edgar J. Kaufmann about bottling milk from the Mountain Top Cooperative for distribution in Pittsburgh. During several trips to Fallingwater, Hagan became intrigued with Wright's design. After purchasing seventy-nine acres of land south of Kaufmann's property in 1953, Hagan commissioned his year-round residence from the architect. Nestled into the side of a mountain, the house has commanding views of the Youghiogheny River Gorge to the northeast.

The Hagans lived in the house until the early 1980s. In 1985, Lord Peter Palumbo, a collector of architecturally significant buildings, bought the well-preserved house. After parts of the structure were ravaged by fire, Palumbo carried out an extensive restoration. In 1996, he opened Kentuck Knob to the public as a historic house museum.

Beth Sholom Synagogue

1954

8231 Old York Rd.
Elkins Park, PA 19027
(215) 887-1342

bethsholompreservation.org

The complex symbolism embodied in the design of this synagogue for a Conservative Jewish congregation is the result of a close collaboration between Rabbi Mortimer J. Cohen and Frank Lloyd Wright. Every element of the design was carefully formulated to reflect some aspect of Jewish faith, history, or religious practice in a building whose character was distinctly contemporary.

The structure's hexagonal plan, according to Wright, mirrors the shape of cupped hands, as if the congregants were "resting in the very hands of God." The translucent pyramidal roof takes the form of a mountain, and the light filtering through its walls symbolizes the gift of the law. The projecting metal spines on the building's exterior represent the seven flames of the menorah.

The 100-foot-high roof is supported by a frame of three 117-foot-long steel beams. The roof's faces are formed from a sandwich of wired glass on the exterior and corrugated plastic on the interior. The main sanctuary can accommodate 1,100 people in seating arranged in triangular sections around two sides of the projecting pulpit. A forty-foot-high concrete monolith, representing the stone tablets given to Moses, forms a dramatic backdrop for the wooden ark containing ten Torah scrolls, one for each of the commandments. A triangular stained-glass "light basket" is suspended from the building's apex. The lower level contains a smaller sanctuary and meeting rooms.

Construction broke ground in November 1954, and the building was dedicated in September 1959, five months after Wright's death. Haskell Culwell, the contractor for Price Tower in Bartlesville, Oklahoma, was the contractor. In 2009 the Beth Sholom Visitor Center opened with interactive new media exhibitions in one of two lower-level lounge spaces Wright designed. A gift shop was created in a former catering kitchen.

Fallingwater

Edgar and Liliane Kaufmann House

1935

1491 Mill Run Rd.
Mill Run, PA 15464
(724) 329-8501

fallingwater.org

The celebrated design of this country house for Pittsburgh department store magnate Edgar J. Kaufmann is the realization of Frank Lloyd Wright's romantic vision of man living in harmony with nature. Native rhododendron and mature trees cover the rugged slopes of the forested glen where a waterfall, fed by a mountain stream, inspired the design of this dwelling.

Determined to build directly over the stream, Wright anchored a series of reinforced-concrete "trays" to the masonry wall and natural rock that form the back of the house. These terraces, extensions of the natural outcroppings, cantilever over the falls and seem to float above the valley floor, blending harmoniously with the rock formations of the streambed below.

Rugged sandstone quarried on the site, concrete, and glass form the exterior and interior fabric of the building. The first-floor entry, living room, and dining room are integrated into a single continuous space. Rather than attempt to move an exceptionally large boulder, Wright simply incorporated it into his design to serve as the hearth. A hatch that opens to a suspended stairway provides ventilation as well as access to the stream below. The upper floors are divided into bedroom suites,

each with its own private terrace. The wood trim throughout is black walnut, and the original furnishings are intact. Expanses of glass and wraparound corner windows dissolve the boundary between interior and exterior spaces, opening the rooms to the surrounding treetops.

In 1938, Wright designed guest quarters set into the hillside directly above the main house. A covered, semicircular walkway links the two structures. In 1963, the Kaufmann family donated the entire property to the Western Pennsylvania Conservancy, which manages regular tours of the property from March through December.

Kalita Humphreys Theater

The New Theater, Dallas Theater Center

1955

3636 Turtle Creek Blvd.
Dallas, TX 75219

info@dallascfa.com

In 1931, Frank Lloyd Wright designed the New Theater for Woodstock, New York, and in 1949, a similar structure for Hartford, Connecticut, but neither was executed. In 1955, commissioned to design a theater in Dallas, Wright proposed adapting his earlier New Theater design for a 1.2-acre site in a park on Turtle Creek Boulevard near the heart of the city. The theater was under construction before Wright's death and was completed in 1959 under the supervision of Taliesin Associated Architects.

The reinforced concrete structure is built into the hillside rock outcroppings and overlooks a winding, wooded creek. Rising dramatically above the creek is a cylindrical concrete drum that contains the stage's fly loft, flanked by circular stair towers. These vertical elements are surrounded by wide, horizontal cantilevered decks over the auditorium spaces, punctuated by cast-in-place concrete windows. With the exception of the round towers, all other forms are designed on a 60- and 120-degree equilateral parallelogram grid.

Wright's concept for the theater freed the stage of its traditional proscenium frame and joined the actors and audience in a unified space. The performance space—a forty-foot-diameter, modified thrust stage—is extended by the use of permanent side stages and upper music

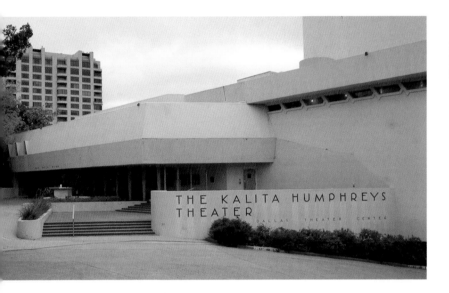

THE KALITA HUMPHREYS
THEATER
DALLAS THEATER CENTER

balconies that flank the panoramic main stage. The house accommodates between 400 and 450 people. A spiral ramp leads to production workshops beneath the auditorium.

Interior changes have included modifying the rake of the floor, extending the technical balconies, and adding loge seating and lighting suspension systems, which have changed sight lines and the natural acoustics. Contemporary modifications involved replacing Wright-designed seating and changing the monochromatic gold color scheme to dark green and red. Exterior changes include the addition of a large stucco rehearsal and office wing in 1968 and a porte cochere that was later enclosed. The large surface parking areas and wide ceremonial entrance have changed the entry experience of Wright's original small grotto entrance. A master plan for restoration has been completed but not yet implemented. The building is open to the public only during performances. For group tours by appointment, contact the Dallas Center for Architecture at info@dallascfa.com.

Pope-Leighey House

Loren Pope House

1939

9000 Richmond Hwy.
Alexandria, VA 22309
(703) 780-4000

woodlawnpopeleighey.org

VIRGINIA

Frank Lloyd Wright designed this 1,200-square-foot house at a total cost of $7,000 after receiving an eloquent letter from Loren Pope, a journalist in Washington, DC, earning a $50-a-week salary. As in most of the Usonian houses Wright designed as an economical solution to suit the needs of the average American family, the interior appears surprisingly spacious despite the modest scale of the building. The flat roof with a cantilevered carport, heated concrete floor slab, recessed lighting, and uniform treatment of the interior and exterior walls are features consistent with other Usonian designs.

The house was sold to Robert and Marjorie Leighey in 1946. The Leigheys were committed to the house for the rest of their lives. In 1963, the structure sat in the path of a highway expansion project and faced demolition. After extensive research, it was donated by Mrs. Leighey to the National Trust for Historic Preservation to ensure its preservation. In 1965 the house was moved fifteen miles away to a hollow within Woodlawn, which was originally part of George Washington's Mount Vernon and still houses a Federal-style mansion designed in 1805 by architect William Thornton. Marjorie Leighey continued to live in the house, allowing periodic tours, until 1983. In 1995, due to the instability of the clay soil, the house had to be moved again, this time only thirty feet uphill, where it still stands today. The house's decor is interpreted to the period of the early 1940s and is complete with the plywood furniture that Pope and the builder constructed to Wright's specifications.

The National Trust for Historic Preservation continues to operate the house as a museum with regular tours most months of the year.

Seth Peterson Cottage
1958

This 880-square-foot building occupies a secluded promontory in one of Wisconsin's most popular state parks, Mirror Lake. The site was originally owned by Seth Peterson, a young man who prevailed upon Frank Lloyd Wright to design a small cottage. Peterson's untimely death in 1960 left the house unfinished. The building was sold, completed, and privately owned until 1966, when it was purchased by the state during an expansion of Mirror Lake State Park.

A central fireplace divides the main living and dining area from the small kitchen, which abuts the single bedroom and bath. The exterior and interior walls as well as the fireplace are locally quarried sandstone. The interior flagstone floors have radiant heating. The flagstone extends beneath the exterior wall to become the floor of the terrace. The windows to the south, east, and west open the interior to the surrounding wooded site and offer a view of the lake. The furnishings were executed from Wright's designs.

Prolonged neglect reduced the building to near ruin before an extensive rehabilitation project was undertaken in 1989. Completed in 1992, the restored cottage was reopened for tours and vacation rental.

Herbert and Katherine Jacobs House

1936

Ranked by the American Institute of Architects as one of the twenty most important residential designs of the twentieth century, the Jacobs House is recognized as the first of Frank Lloyd Wright's Usonian houses. The 1,550-square-foot, one-story, L-shaped house was designed and built for a family of ordinary means, a response to the evolving economic and social conditions of the country during the Great Depression and to the era of expanding suburbs in the United States.

The house incorporates the most basic forms and materials to create small, economical spaces and elegant but minimalist design. It was in the Jacobs House that Wright first used his "sandwich-wall" construction, which consists of three layers: interior and exterior layers of horizontal pine board with a vertical pine-board core.

The Usonian house type was planned for maximum privacy, turning a nearly solid wall to the street. By siting the Jacobs House close to the edge of the lot, the driveway could be shorter to allocate more space to the garden. A dramatically cantilevered carport, the first that Wright designed, projects from the house and signals the location of two entrances, one leading into the living room and the other into the bedroom wing. The efficient spatial design is warmed by the reliable, simple

materials, brick and gleaming wood. The walls are largely solid except for bands of clerestory windows. In the living room the comparatively high ceiling and a series of full-height glazed doors opening onto the terrace and garden create a sense of continuous flow between indoors and out and offer an impression of spaciousness rarely found in houses of this size.

The house is privately owned and maintained as a residence; it is open selectively by appointment for public tours.

■ Unitarian Meeting House

1947

900 University Bay Dr.
Madison, WI 53705
(608) 233-9774

fusmadison.org/landmark

Frank Lloyd Wright described the Unitarian Meeting House as a hilltop "country church" to be constructed of native stone and wood with a copper roof. Unitarian in character, he said, not simply an aggregation of steeple, meeting house, and parsonage, the mass of the building itself would give the impression of unity and aspiration.

Commissioned in 1946, the church took five years to build and cost more than three times Wright's initial estimate of $60,000, even though church members worked as construction volunteers on weekends. A herculean effort was required to haul more than one thousand tons of limestone to the site from a quarry thirty miles away. Wright, too, felt personally invested in the project. His parents were among the earliest First Unitarian Society members, and he had officially joined the organization in 1938. He accepted a minimal fee, offered the assistance of Taliesin apprentices, and helped to raise funds by giving two lectures.

The design of the building is governed by a diamond module. The form is evident in the incised pattern in the concrete floor, the shape of the auditorium and hearth room, the zigzag interior wall of the loggia, and the stone piers and planters. The auditorium, with its soaring ceiling and glass prow, in combination with the adjacent hearth room,

can accommodate 340 people. A loggia leads to the west living room, where social functions are held. The auditorium and hearth room contain portable and collapsible benches and tables of Wright's design. The framing of the copper-clad roof, the building's most distinctive feature, set Wright at odds with local building commissioners who doubted its structural stability. The interior ceiling is actually much lower and does not conform to the angle of the exterior roof. An education wing was added in 1964 and another hexagonal wing in 1990, both designed by Taliesin Associated Architects. A third addition (which replaced much of the 1990 wing) was completed in 2008, adding a new five-hundred-seat auditorium. The Wright-designed space was renovated and its original colors were restored at that time.

Arthur Richards American System-Built Houses

1915

2714–34 W. Burnham St.
1835 S. Layton Blvd.
Milwaukee, WI 53215
(608) 287-0339

wrightinmilwaukee.org

Beginning in 1911, companies connected to Arthur L. Richards, a Milwaukee real estate developer, had engaged Frank Lloyd Wright to design several projects, including an unbuilt hotel in Madison and the since-demolished Hotel Geneva in Lake Geneva, Wisconsin. By November 1916, Richards had entered into an agreement with Wright to design a series of houses that would be marketed under the name American System-Built Houses. The construction materials and plans would be packaged in kits and shipped by rail throughout the country. Richards was also to recruit a sales and distribution channel of builders and developers, and to create advertising materials. He appears to have focused his efforts on Chicago and a few other Midwestern cities.

This is a unique project undertaken by Wright that exemplifies his lifelong interest in housing every American in beautiful, reasonably priced, innovative homes of his design. Wright and Richards anticipated that the American System-Built Houses would be wildly successful. Unfortunately, the United States' entry into World War I diverted the attention of the buying public and also redirected building materials to meeting wartime demands. Housing starts ground to a halt, and only about twenty American System-Built Houses were built. Wright shifted

his focus to the Imperial Hotel commission, and his business relationship with Richards unraveled.

The six structures on Milwaukee's Burnham Street and Layton Boulevard were constructed between October 1915 and July 1916. Other examples were built on scattered sites throughout the Midwest. The Burnham Street structures consist of four two-story stucco-clad duplexes with flat roofs, and two one-story cottages of different designs. All of the houses have been altered. Most noticeable is the addition of precast stone, a porch enclosure, and metal-tile roofing at 1835 S. Layton. Less evident are interior alterations and the replacement of all exterior surfaces.

Two of the houses have been meticulously restored and are open for regular docent-led tours. One is in private hands and available as a vacation rental. The nonprofit organization Frank Lloyd Wright Wisconsin is actively fundraising for ongoing restoration projects with the goal of restoring all of the homes and eventually opening an education and visitors center.

■ SC Johnson Administration Building and Research Tower

1936 and 1943

1525 Howe St.
Racine, WI 53403

scjohnson.com/visit

WISCONSIN

In 1936, third-generation SC Johnson president and CEO Herbert Fisk Johnson Jr. commissioned Frank Lloyd Wright to design the company's new headquarters. Johnson envisioned a building that would provide a functional, pleasant working environment as well as project a modern corporate image. When completed in 1939, the Administration Building was hailed in *LIFE* magazine as "a truer glimpse of the shape of things to come."

To block out the surrounding industrial landscape, the streamlined, curving brick building face was designed without conventional window openings. With no views of nature to frame, Wright created an interior forest of slender, tapering dendriform columns of high-strength concrete and steel mesh that widen to support the concrete pads carrying the weight of the roof. The base has a diameter of only nine inches, compared to the top diameter of 18½ feet. Wright infamously exhibited the surprising strength of the columns during construction by having sixty tons of sand—five times what the state required for the construction permit—piled atop one.

Wright's use of translucent glass tubing instead of transparent window glass was equally unprecedented. Forty-three miles of layered Pyrex tubing formed the clerestories beneath the mezzanine and below the cornice line, as well as the skylit openings around the column capitals. Shadowless, natural light floods the interior, creating a workplace Wright claimed would be "as inspiring to live and work in as any cathedral ever was to worship in."

The brick used in both interior and exterior walls was custom-made in two hundred shapes to produce the necessary curves and angles. The mortar joints were raked to preserve the streamlined, horizontal effect of the masonry walls.

In 1943, Johnson returned to Wright to design new quarters for the company's research and development division. The resulting Research Tower is connected to the main building by a covered bridge. It is one of only two tall buildings Wright ever constructed and one of the tallest structures ever built on the cantilever principle. It stands 153 feet tall, and the building's central core, which is 13 feet in diameter and extends 54 feet deep into the ground, supports all fifteen floors. Reinforced concrete slabs cantilevered from the core form the alternating square floors and circular balconies. A central shaft contains the stairway, elevator, and mechanical systems. The tower was closed in 1982, but SC Johnson continued to maintain it. In 2013 the company undertook an extensive restoration, and in the spring of 2014 Wright's tower opened to the public for the first time, with two open floors now exhibiting both the history of the architecture and the famous household products developed inside it.

Regular guided tours of the SC Johnson campus are available to the public and can be combined with tours of Wingspread, the nearby house Wright built for Johnson.

A. D. German Warehouse

1915

300 S. Church St.
Richland Center, WI 53581
(608) 604-5034

adgermanwarehouse.org

Albert D. German, a Richland Center wholesale commodities dealer, planned to expand his business and commissioned Frank Lloyd Wright to design a new warehouse. Wright conceived a four-story, fifty-by-eighty-foot structure that rises from a concrete base. Its red-brick exterior is crowned by an intricate frieze of contrasting gray concrete that incorporates fifty-four windows into its geometric design.

The flat-slab structure is designed in a grid of massive, steel-reinforced concrete columns with flaring capitals that carry the weight of the floor and roof. The capitals of six columns were designed with decorative motifs similar to the exterior frieze. Double-brick-wall construction provided adequate insulation to create a cold-storage environment without the need for mechanical refrigeration. Elimination of interior walls allowed maximum freedom of usable space.

By 1921, the original estimated construction cost of $30,000 had reached $125,000, forcing German to halt work on the warehouse and eventually lose the building through bankruptcy proceedings. Subsequent owners leased the building for storage and small-scale manufacturing. Renovation in the 1970s and 1980s added a small theater on the first level and a gift shop, respectively. In 2014, after two years of combined local and national preservation efforts, local philanthropists purchased the structure and donated it to the A. D. German Warehouse Conservancy for restoration and rehabilitation.

The warehouse is open for tours on Sundays seasonally with additional times by appointment.

Frank Lloyd Wright Visitor Center
5607 County Rd. C
Spring Green, WI 53588
(608) 588-7900

taliesinpreservation.org

Taliesin ■

Begun 1911

Frank Lloyd Wright spent the summers of his adolescence roaming the Wisconsin farmland owned by his mother's family, fostering an appreciation for nature that would inspire his philosophy of organic architecture. In 1911, he returned to build a new house. He named the site Taliesin, Welsh for "shining brow," referring to the crest of the hill. A residence, farm, studio, and school, Taliesin evolved over nearly five decades. Partially destroyed by fire in 1914 and 1925, the house was rebuilt and enlarged each time.

The garden walls, terraces, house, and chimneys were constructed of yellow limestone from a nearby quarry. The long layers of stone simulate the natural strata of nearby outcroppings. The sand-colored upper walls recede beneath deep eaves, and the rooflines were designed to conform to the slope of surrounding hills.

The interior demonstrates Wright's masterful orchestration of light, form, texture, and color in a harmonious composition. The entrance is through a low, narrow passage leading to the dramatic, light-filled living room. Parallel bands of cypress trim accentuate striking changes in ceiling height, and windows provide expansive views of the countryside.

Wright designed buildings on adjoining land for his family beginning in 1887 with the Hillside Home Building, the first building he designed

for the Hillside Home School—a boarding school administered by his aunts Nell and Jenny Lloyd Jones. Wright demolished that building in 1950. The Romeo and Juliet Windmill, built in 1897 and reconstructed in 1992, pumped water to the school. In 1902–3, Wright constructed a new Hillside Home School of ashlar-cut sandstone and oak, containing a gymnasium, laboratory, drawing studio, assembly hall, and classrooms. In 1932, he converted the gymnasium to a theater and constructed a large drafting room and dormitory rooms to accommodate his architectural training program, which still operates today as the Frank Lloyd Wright School of Architecture.

In 1907, Wright designed the Prairie-style house Tan-y-deri ("under the oaks") for his sister Jane and her husband, Andrew Porter. The Midway Barns were constructed beginning in the 1920s to house livestock. In 1953 Wright designed the structure housing the current visitor center as a restaurant to be frequented by guests at Taliesin. The project languished until a resort developer purchased the plans and constructed the restaurant in 1967. In 1993 it was converted to house the visitor center from which all Taliesin tours depart. The Riverview Spring Green Restaurant now operates on site.

Unity Chapel ■

1886

This modest, shingle-sided structure designed by Chicago architect Joseph L. Silsbee and located near Spring Green, Wisconsin, was frequently referred to by Wright as his "first work."

Unity Chapel was commissioned by Wright's family, the Lloyd Joneses, who settled the rural Wyoming Valley land in the mid-1860s. Wright's contribution to the chapel was reported in *Unity* magazine in 1886 thusly: "A boy architect belonging to the family looked after this interior." Presumably this included designing and perhaps helping to install its patterned wood ceilings and selecting the olive green and terra-cotta wall colors, according to Wright scholar Mary Jane Hamilton. The space is divided into an auditorium and parlor, separated by a decorative curtain, and small kitchen. The chapel served as a worship center, community meeting house, school, and gathering place for family and friends. It is surrounded by the family graveyard.

Today the chapel is opened selectively for weddings, family gatherings, funerals, musical programs, and summer services.

Wyoming Valley School Cultural Arts Center

Wyoming Valley Schoolhouse

1956

6306 State Rd. 23
Spring Green, WI 53588
(608) 588-2544

wyomingvalleyschool
.blogspot.com

In honor of his mother, Anna Lloyd-Jones Wright, who had been a kindergarten teacher, Frank Lloyd Wright donated his design for this schoolhouse and 2½ acres of land a few miles from Taliesin to the Wyoming School District. The building was derived from Wright's 1926 Kinder-symphonies project, a series of playhouses for the Oak Park Playground Association. The schoolhouse consists of two classrooms, an auditorium, two bathrooms, a kitchen, and a teachers' room. The main assembly room contains a central fireplace on a raised stage and a band of clerestory windows at the top, flooding the space with daylight. Wright's early drawings showed the structure fronted with native limestone similar to Taliesin, but standard concrete block was used in the final construction.

The school opened in 1958 with its first class of forty-six students in first through eighth grade. The school was closed in 1990, and in 2010 it was donated to the nonprofit Wyoming Valley School Inc. and converted into an educational center offering arts and cultural workshops, performances, and lectures to residents of the Wyoming Valley and surrounding areas.

Still Bend ■

Bernard and Fern
Schwartz House

1939

Bernard and Fern Schwartz commissioned Frank Lloyd Wright to design their riverfront home in 1939. The house is based upon the September 1938 LIFE magazine competition entitled "Eight Houses for Modern Living," in which Wright was among eight architects tapped to design a "dream house" for a typical American family with an annual income of $2,000 to $10,000. Wright's design was intended for the Blackburn family of Edina, Minnesota, who instead built a more traditional house. The Schwartzes proceeded with construction of a slightly modified plan the following year.

Named Still Bend for the bend in the East Twin River, which flows through the rear of the property, the Usonian house is a two-story, flat-roofed structure made of brick, wood, and glass. The two-story section houses the bedrooms and includes a balcony that overlooks the one-and-a-half-story living space. A carport is cantilevered from the bedroom wing toward the street. Wright apprentice Edgar Tafel supervised construction of the house and added hidden steel supports to the structure without Wright's knowledge.

The house remains privately owned but is available for tours and overnight rentals by reservation.

Annunciation Greek Orthodox Church

1956

■

The Greek Orthodox community of Milwaukee commissioned Frank Lloyd Wright to design its church in 1956 in suburban Wauwatosa. Wright died five weeks before the start of construction, and supervision of the project fell to his apprentice John U. Ottenheimer. Although Wright's design represents a distinct departure from traditional Byzantine church architecture, he retained the domed space and incorporated the symbols of the Greek Orthodox faith in his two-level plan, including a cross inscribed in a circle. Four equidistant, reinforced-concrete piers support the structure and define the cross on the main floor. The cross symbol also serves as ornament throughout the sanctuary.

The main-level space accommodates 240 congregants; circular staircases lead to additional seating for 560 above. The sanctuary has no interior supports to obstruct the view of the parishioners, and no one sits more than sixty feet from the altar. The lower level of the church contains a circular banquet hall connected to an underground classroom wing. Gold anodized aluminum is the principal metal used throughout the building.

Wright designed a dome 106 feet in diameter, with a maximum height of 45 feet, to sit atop the structure. The dome's concrete shell is

not fixed but floats on thousands of steel bearings contained in a circular channel beam that caps the outer wall. Originally covered with blue ceramic tile, the exterior of the dome is now covered with a synthetic resin. Semicircular windows (with stained glass not designed by Wright) and transparent glass spheres crown the upper wall and allow light to enter the church.

The church maintains weekly services that are open to the public.

33 E. 4 Mile Rd.
Wind Point, WI 53402

scjohnson.com/visit

Wingspread

Herbert and Irene
Johnson House

1937

After Herbert Fisk Johnson Jr., grandson of SC Johnson founder Samuel Curtis Johnson, commissioned Frank Lloyd Wright to design his company's new headquarters in Racine, Wisconsin, he enlisted the architect again to design his new family house, Wingspread, on a secluded, wooded parcel nearby. Wright apprentice John Lautner supervised the construction, which occurred at the same time as the SC Johnson Administration Building. Both were completed in 1939. Wingspread would come to be, as architectural historian Henry-Russell Hitchcock quoted Wright as saying, "the last of the Prairie houses."

Constructed of brick, stone, wood, and glass, the house comprises four wings that emanate from a central core in a pinwheel configuration. The central core and one wing are two stories in height whereas the remaining three wings are one story. At the center of the core is an elongated masonry mass containing four fireplaces on the first floor and one additional fireplace on the second-floor balcony. Wright called the center hall the "wigwam." Three bands of clerestory windows taper up to the roof, where a spiral staircase leads to a chimney-top glass enclosure dubbed the "crow's nest." Wright designed this unique feature for Johnson's children to watch their father approach in his private plane.

In 1959, the Johnsons gave the house and grounds to The Johnson Foundation, which today operates an educational conference center encompassing Wingspread, the Henry L. Eggers–designed house Johnson had built overlooking Wingspread in 1959, and a forty-two-room guesthouse completed in 2002 to provide luxury accommodations to conference attendees.

Imperial Hotel Entrance Hall and Lobby Reconstruction

1913–22

The Museum Meiji-Mura
1 Uchiyama, Inuyama-shi
Aichi, 484-0000
Japan

meijimura.com/english

The Imperial Hotel in Tokyo was one of the largest and most elaborate commissions of Frank Lloyd Wright's career. He made his first personal visit to Japan in 1905 at the age of thirty-seven, and the influence of Japanese architecture can be felt in numerous Wright designs in the United States.

In his plans for the Imperial Hotel, Wright rejected the Japanese trend of using European-style building materials in favor of locally sourced brick and steel-reinforced concrete. *Oya-ishi* (Oya stone), the distinctive Japanese rock created from lava and ash, was used for ornamental accents and sculptural pieces throughout the hotel. At the front of the symmetrical structure were the multitiered lobby, a restaurant, and other public spaces. A seven-story building at the back contained a cabaret, theater, and a double-height banquet hall. Two guest-room wings stretched along interior gardens on either side. Lightweight copper tiles covered the roof.

Wright's structural innovations—unprecedented in Japan at the time and designed to minimize damage from earthquakes and fires—proved controversial, but also prescient. On the fateful day the opening of the completed building was to be celebrated, September 1, 1923, the Great Kanto Earthquake devastated Tokyo. Although the expansive hotel suffered minor damage, it famously remained standing after the powerful quake leveled many of the city's buildings.

For decades the Imperial Hotel hosted elite travelers to Japan, but the effects of World War II bombings, subway construction under the hotel, deferred maintenance, and the need for more rooms led owners to demolish the building and build a new high-rise hotel on the site. Demolition began in 1967 and was completed in 1968. A portion of the hotel's decorative Oya stone and other finishing materials were preserved and moved some 220 miles away to the Museum Meiji-Mura, an open-air museum that displays more than sixty buildings preserved from Japan's Meiji Period (1868–1912). The entrance hall, lobby, and reflecting pool of the Imperial Hotel were reconstructed and opened in 1985.

Yodoko Guest House ■

Yamamura House

1918

Frank Lloyd Wright designed this four-level house, which sits atop a steep, wooded hill with views over the city and Kobe Bay, as a summer house for eighth-generation sake brewer Tazaemon Yamamura. Arata Endo, Wright's trusted collaborator in Japan, fleshed out Wright's plans and added three *tatami*-mat rooms with *shoji* sliding panels and, on the salon's clerestory level, tiny doors inspired by the transoms of traditional Japanese houses to allow cross breezes, according to scholar Karen Severns. Construction began in 1923 and was supervised by Endo and Makoto Minami, another Wright disciple who worked on the Imperial Hotel. It was completed in 1924.

The front entrance is hidden under the portico at the top of a steep driveway. Stairs lead to the second-floor salon, lined with built-in couches beneath wide windows on both the eastern and western sides of the room. The three connected Japanese-style rooms are located on the third floor, and a Western-style dining room with a spacious balcony is on the fourth. The stonework on the interior and exterior is *Oya-ishi*, a rock created from lava and ash and quarried only in a small area of Utsunomiya in Tochigi Prefecture. Easily carved with decorative patterns, the stone was also used extensively on the Imperial Hotel and uniquely characterizes Wright's work in Japan.

In 1947, the house was purchased by the Osaka-based company Yodogawa Steel Works and used first as a residence for the company president and later as employee apartments. In 1974, the house was designated as an Important Cultural Property, the Japanese equivalent of a national landmark. Restoration work was completed in the mid-1980s and the house was opened to the public as Yodoko Guest House in 1989. In 1995 the building suffered damage in the Great Hanshin-Awaji Earthquake, but by 1998 repair work had been completed and the house museum was again open to the public.

Myonichikan ■

Jiyu Gakuen School

1921

In 1921, when Frank Lloyd Wright was working on the Imperial Hotel in Tokyo, he was approached by the founders of Jiyu Gakuen (freedom school), Yoshikazu and Motoko Hani, to design a building for their all-girls school in Ikebukuro, a district of Tokyo. They sought an architectural expression that reflected the Christian-oriented school's creed of self-reliance and egalitarianism.

The design—a collaboration between Wright and his chief assistant on the Imperial Hotel, Arata Endo—is a large U-shaped plan with three long buildings built around an open courtyard bounded by cherry trees. At the center is a double-height main hall with expansive views of the front lawn. The construction is wood frame and stucco, with the distinctive Japanese volcanic *Oya-ishi* (Oya stone) at the base, capped by a copper roof. Diagonal wood strips are used to create simple decorative patterns on windows throughout the building. Wright-designed furniture scaled to the children's size can be found throughout.

Endo completed the building after Wright's departure from Japan and designed a three-hundred-seat auditorium addition. By 1934, the school had moved to a new campus outside of Tokyo designed by Endo and his son, Raku Endo, known as Wright's last Japanese apprentice.

By the early 1990s, the Wright building, falling into disrepair, was used mostly for alumni events. It became known as Myonichikan (house of tomorrow). When the land on which it sat was estimated to be valued at more than $200 million, the building was threatened with demolition. Remembering the fate that befell Wright's masterful Imperial Hotel in 1967, an international coalition of preservationists came together to raise public awareness of the last remaining Wright-designed building in Tokyo. More than twenty Japanese and American supporters, including the Frank Lloyd Wright Building Conservancy, signed a full-page advertisement in the *New York Times* asking Americans to write to President Bush ahead of his planned visit to Japan. An international symposium in 1992 assembled prominent Wright scholars and preservation experts in Japan to focus on the preservation of Myonichikan as a cultural bridge between the United States and Japan. In 1997, Japanese officials announced the building would be designated as an Important Cultural Property (similar to a National Historic Landmark). After a two-year restoration, Myonichikan opened to the public in 2001 for regular tours and event rentals.

For those interested in visiting buildings designed by Frank Lloyd Wright in a specific area, the following daylong or multiday excursions are suggested. Planning in advance is required, as some Wright sites operate as house museums with regular hours while others have limited hours or require reservations or special accommodations for public touring. Please check with each site to confirm hours, tour schedules and availability, fees, and directions before making travel plans.

ARIZONA

■ **Taliesin West**
Scottsdale PAGE 22

■ **ASU Gammage**
Tempe PAGE 24

The Phoenix-Scottsdale area is home to Frank Lloyd Wright's winter residence and studio, Taliesin West, and one of his late works, the ASU Gammage auditorium. Taliesin West has an extensive year-round tour program—opt for the three-hour Behind-the-Scenes Tour and consider the Desert "Shelter" Tour to see the unique shelters designed by students at the Frank Lloyd Wright School of Architecture. If visiting in the summer, plan an early outing to avoid the heat.

After leaving Taliesin West, drive past the 125-foot spire, built in 2004, that was based on Wright's unbuilt 1957 design for the Arizona State Capitol building. Make a stop at First Christian Church, which was built by Taliesin Associated Architects in 1971–78 based on portions of Wright's 1950 design for the Southwest Christian Seminary. The church offers Sunday morning services, and an informal look at its interior may be possible if staff is available during weekday office hours.

Plan to include a performance at ASU Gammage to experience the three-thousand-seat concert hall designed by Wright, or call ahead to arrange a tour. Then treat yourself to a night at the Arizona Biltmore, a luxury resort hotel designed by former Wright draftsman Albert Chase McArthur in 1927. Wanting to incorporate Wright's textile-block slab method of construction for the hotel, McArthur retained Wright as a consultant for technical assistance for several months. The precise extent of Wright's involvement remains unclear, though his influence is widely felt throughout the historic portion of the hotel complex.

See also

FRANK LLOYD WRIGHT SPIRE
Frank Lloyd Wright Blvd.
and Scottsdale Rd., Scottsdale

ARIZONA BILTMORE
2400 E. Missouri Ave., Phoenix
(602) 955-6600
arizonabiltmore.com

FIRST CHRISTIAN CHURCH
6750 N. 7th Ave., Phoenix
(602) 246-9206
fccphx.com

146 Begin your trip in downtown San Francisco with a visit to Wright's only building in the city, the V. C. Morris Gift Shop. Originally designed for a California businessman and later occupied by other retailers and an art gallery, the building was acquired by new owners in 2015. A designer menswear boutique plans to open in the space in late spring 2017 (search online for opening hours). Next, drive about forty miles south to Stanford to see the Paul and Jean Hanna House, one of Wright's most elaborate Usonian designs. Arranging a tour of the building, which is owned by Stanford University, will require careful planning as there is currently no regular tour schedule, but even a viewing of the exterior and landscaping is worth the drive for most Wright enthusiasts.

The next day, head north from San Francisco over the Golden Gate Bridge to the Marin County Civic Center, designed late in Wright's career and completed after his death. Be sure to stop at the fairgrounds area, near the auditorium designed by Taliesin Associated Architects, for a picture-perfect view of Wright's sprawling complex across a lagoon. Before beginning one of the regularly scheduled docent-led tours of the civic center, take a peek inside the Wright-designed post office, which is located between the fairgrounds and the main entrance to the civic center Administration Building. Adventurous travelers may want to continue some two hundred miles north to see Pilgrim Congregational Church in Redding. This lesser-known building, constructed after Wright's death, represents only a portion of the plan he envisioned for the congregation.

NORTHERN ILLINOIS

Frank Lloyd Wright buildings, including some of his earliest designs, are plentiful in northern Illinois. If starting from Chicago, consider taking a day to drive about ninety miles northwest of the city for a regular tour (currently offered only on the weekends) of the Kenneth and Phyllis Laurent House, Wright's only design for a wheelchair-bound client. On the way back to Chicago, stop at the small Pettit Memorial Chapel in the Belvidere Cemetery and consider a detour through Geneva to see the Fabyan Villa. A detour to the northern suburb of Glencoe offers a Wright-designed bridge and an opportunity to stroll past several private houses he designed in the Ravine Bluffs neighborhood.

Wright's Chicago work stretches from the city's northernmost neighborhood, where the Emil and Anna Bach House is available for tours as well as overnight stays, to the renowned Frederick and Lora Robie House, which has frequent regular tours, on the city's South Side. Downtown you'll find the Charnley-Persky House, which Wright worked on while employed by Louis Sullivan, and the Rookery Building, an 1888 Burnham and Root building with a publicly accessible central light court remodeled by Wright.

About ten miles west of the city is Oak Park, home to the largest concentration of Wright-designed buildings in the world. Book a tour of the Frank Lloyd Wright Home and Studio and add on a self-guided or interpreter-led walking tour of Oak Park to see the exteriors of some of the distinctive private houses Wright designed in the town where he lived and worked for twenty years. Unity Temple, scheduled to re-open to the public in 2017 following a restoration, is another must-see design, and remnants of Wright's work can be viewed in the Francisco Terrace Archway reconstruction and the Waller Gates. A 1969 replica of a fountain sculpture on which Wright collaborated with sculptor Richard Bock sits at the entrance to Scoville Park not far from where the original, designed in 1903, was demolished.

See also

SCOVILLE PARK FOUNTAIN
Oak Park Ave. and Lake St.,
Oak Park

SOUTHERN ILLINOIS
AND ST. LOUIS, MISSOURI

After visiting Wright's Chicago-area sites, enthusiasts can expand their Illinois itineraries south to Missouri. Begin about sixty miles south of downtown Chicago with a regular docent-led tour of the B. Harley and Anna Bradley House, recognized as one of Wright's first Prairie houses. Continue west to Dwight, where during business hours you can view the inside of the Wright-designed First National Bank of Dwight. From there, it's about 120 miles to Wright's extravagant Dana-Thomas House in Springfield; allow ninety minutes for a regular docent-led tour of Wright's largest surviving Prairie house, now a state-owned house museum. During business hours you can pay a visit to the reconstructed Wright-designed library gifted to the city by the house's original owner, Susan Lawrence Dana. The next day, make the 110-mile drive from Springfield to St. Louis, Missouri, to see Wright's Usonian house in Ebsworth Park, which offers tours by appointment.

150 A trip to western Pennsylvania affords an ultimate Wright-centered weekend. Plan ahead to stay overnight at the Wright-designed Donald and Elizabeth Duncan House, which was moved to Acme from its original location in the Chicago suburbs, and get a full tour of the surrounding Polymath Park, which includes two houses designed by Wright apprentice Peter Berndtson. The park will soon be home to the Wright-designed R. W. Lindholm House, a 1952 Usonian that was moved from its endangered site in Cloquet, Minnesota, to be reconstructed and preserved at Polymath Park in 2017.

A tour of Fallingwater is essential for any Wright enthusiast. Opt for one of the small-group, in-depth tours, but reserve early as they fill up months in advance. Just seven miles south is Kentuck Knob, which also offers regular tours. If time allows for a 275-mile drive east, a tour of Wright's landmark Beth Sholom Synagogue is well worth the journey, and fifty miles north of Elkins Park you will find the reconstructed library from the Francis and Mary Little House II in the Allentown Art Museum.

WISCONSIN

As is the case in northern Illinois, the options for visiting Frank Lloyd Wright buildings in Wisconsin abound. Intrepid Wright enthusiasts with ample time to commit could pair Illinois and Wisconsin excursions, as Racine, Wisconsin, is only some seventy-five miles north of downtown Chicago—and home to one of Wright's towering achievements, the SC Johnson Administration Building and Research Tower. A tour of this famed office complex can be coupled with a visit to nearby Wingspread, the house Wright designed for SC Johnson's then-CEO, Herbert Fisk Johnson Jr.

About twenty-five miles north of Racine, see Wright's experiments with prefabricated housing on a tour of the Arthur Richards American System-Built Houses in Milwaukee. Then head to the near suburb of Wauwatosa to view his Annunciation Greek Orthodox Church, or attend a public service there. If an overnight stay in a Wright-designed Usonian house in a quiet lakeside town appeals, book a night or two at Still Bend, ninety miles north in Two Rivers, or check the site's tour schedule if staying over isn't an option.

The next leg of a Wisconsin trip begins eighty miles west of Milwaukee in Madison, where a visit to the Unitarian Meeting House is a must, and a tour of the Herbert and Katherine Jacobs House, Wright's first Usonian, is possible with advance planning. Madison is also home to Monona Terrace, a large convention center constructed from 1994–97. It was proposed by Wright as early as 1938, with designs modified by him as late as 1959. Monona Terrace's interior was reconfigured by Taliesin Associated Architects, Wright's successor firm, which eventually completed the building, but the exterior profile and relationship to its prominent site on Lake Monona are largely consistent with Wright's 1959 design.

Another opportunity for an off-the-beaten-path overnight stay (or simply a tour, if one has been arranged) can be found at the Seth Peterson Cottage about fifty miles northwest of Madison in Mirror Lake State Park. Following a detour through Richland Center, if a tour of Wright's A. D. German Warehouse has been arranged, drive about twenty-five miles to Spring Green to see Wright's own home and studio at Taliesin, as well as his Wyoming Valley School Cultural Arts Center and Unity Chapel. A variety of Taliesin tours are offered, but consider the four-hour Estate Tour, which traverses the grounds on foot to view each of the property's Wright-designed structures.

See also

MONONA TERRACE
1 John Nolen Dr., Madison
(608) 261-4000
mononaterrace.com

154

Sites are labeled on the maps according to page number

MILES 100 200 300

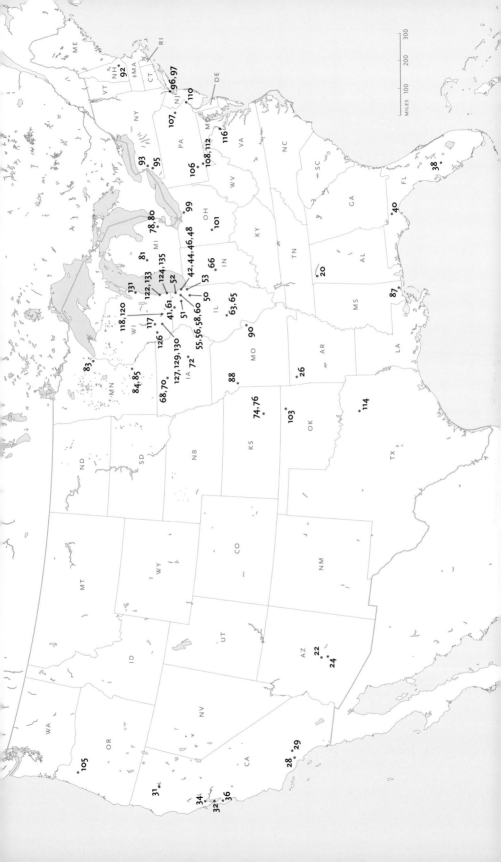

SITE INDEX

ARCHIVES DIRECTORY

ARIZONA

The Frank Lloyd Wright Collections
The Frank Lloyd Wright Foundation
Taliesin West
12621 N. Frank Lloyd Wright Blvd.
Scottsdale, AZ 85261
(480) 860-2700, ext. 5353
franklloydwright.org

CALIFORNIA

The Getty Research Institute
1200 Getty Center Dr.,
    Ste. 1100
Los Angeles, CA 90049
(310) 440-7300
getty.edu/research/

DISTRICT OF COLUMBIA

Archives of American Art
Smithsonian Institution
750 9th St. N.W.
Victor Building, Ste. 2200
Washington, DC 20001
(202) 633-7940
aaa.si.edu/

Manuscript Reading Room
Library of Congress
James Madison Memorial
    Building, Rm. 101
101 Independence Ave. S.E.
Washington, DC 20540
(202) 707-5387
loc.gov/rr/mss/

Prints and Photographs Division
Historic American Buildings Survey
Library of Congress
James Madison Memorial
    Building, Rm. 337
101 Independence Ave. S.E.
Washington, DC 20540
(202) 707-6394
loc.gov/rr/print/

ILLINOIS

Frank Lloyd Wright Trust
Frank Lloyd Wright Home and Studio
951 Chicago Ave.
Oak Park, IL 60302
(312) 994-4000
flwright.org

Oak Park Public Library
834 Lake St.
Oak Park, IL 60301
(708) 383-8200
oppl.org

Ryerson & Burnham Libraries
Art Institute of Chicago
111 S. Michigan Ave.
Chicago, IL 60603
(312) 443-7292
artic.edu

NEW YORK

Avery Architectural and Fine Arts Library
Columbia University
1172 Amsterdam Ave.
New York, NY 10027
(212) 854-6199
library.columbia
    .edu/locations/avery

The Buffalo History Museum
Research Library
1 Museum Ct.
Buffalo, NY 14216
(716) 873-9644
buffalohistory.org

University Archives
The State University of New York at Buffalo
420 Capen Hall
Buffalo, NY 14260
(716) 645-2916
library.buffalo.edu/archives/

Lily Auchincloss Study Center for Architecture and Design
Museum of Modern Art
11 W. 53rd St.
New York, NY 10019
(212) 708-9542
moma.org

Department of American Decorative Art
The Metropolitan Museum of Art
Fifth Ave. and 82nd St.
New York, NY 10028
(212) 535-7110
metmuseum.org

WISCONSIN

Library-Archives Division
Wisconsin Historical Society
816 State St.
Madison, WI 53706
(608) 264-6535
wisconsinhistory.org

Milwaukee Art Museum
700 N. Art Museum Dr.
Milwaukee, WI 53202
(414) 224-3200
mam.org

CANADA

Canadian Centre for Architecture
1920 Rue Baile
Montréal, Québec
H3H 2S6 Canada
(514) 939-7026
cca.qc.ca

SELECTED BIBLIOGRAPHY

Abernathy, Ann, and John Thorpe, *The Oak Park Home and Studio of Frank Lloyd Wright* (Oak Park, IL: Frank Lloyd Wright Home and Studio Foundation, 1988).

Brooks, H. Allen, *The Prairie School: Frank Lloyd Wright and His Midwest Contemporaries* (New York: W.W. Norton & Company, 2005).

Bruegmann, Robert. **"The Rookery Renaissance: Preservation's Touchstone,"** *Inland Architect* (July/August 1992): 50–57.

Buffalo Architectural Guidebook Corporation, *Buffalo Architecture: A Guide* (Cambridge, MA: MIT Press, 1981).

Connors, Joseph, *The Robie House of Frank Lloyd Wright* (Chicago: University of Chicago Press, 1984).

Gebhard, David, *Romanza: The California Architecture of Frank Lloyd Wright* (San Francisco: Chronicle Books, 1988).

Green, Aaron G., *An Architecture for Democracy: The Marin County Civic Center* (San Francisco: Grendon Publishing, 1990).

Gurda, John, *New World Odyssey: Annunciation Greek Orthodox Church and Frank Lloyd Wright* (Milwaukee: Milwaukee Hellenic Community, 1986).

Haight, Deborah S. and Peter F. Blume, *Frank Lloyd Wright: The Library from the Francis W. Little House* (Allentown, PA: Allentown Art Museum, 1978).

Hallmark, Donald P., *Frank Lloyd Wright's Dana-Thomas House* (Springfield, IL: Illinois Historic Preservation Agency, 1990).

Hanna, Paul R. and Jean S. Hanna, *Frank Lloyd Wright's Hanna House* (Carbondale, IL: Southern Illinois University Press, 1987).

Heckscher, Morrison and Elizabeth G. Miller, *An Architect and His Client: Frank Lloyd Wright and Francis W. Little* (New York: Metropolitan Museum of Art, 1973).

Hitchcock, Henry-Russell, *In the Nature of Materials* (New York: Duell, Sloan, and Pearce, 1942; reprint New York: Da Capo, 1973).

Hoffman, Donald, *Frank Lloyd Wright's Fallingwater: The House and its History* (New York: Dover, 1978).

Levine, Neil, *The Architecture of Frank Lloyd Wright* (Princeton, NJ: Princeton University Press, 1996).

Lipman, Jonathan, *Frank Lloyd Wright and the Johnson Wax Buildings* (New York: Rizzoli, 1986).

Manson, Grant Carpenter, *Frank Lloyd Wright to 1910: The First Golden Age* (New York: Wiley, 1979).

McCoy, Robert E. **"Rock Crest/ Rock Glen: Prairie Planning In Iowa,"** *Prairie School Review* 5 (1968): 5–34.

Pfeiffer, Bruce Brooks, *Frank Lloyd Wright: Complete Works,* vols. 1–3 (Los Angeles: Taschen America, 2009–11).

Pfeiffer, Bruce Brooks, ed., *Letters to Clients: Frank Lloyd Wright* (Fresno, Calif.: California State University, 1986).

Quinan, Jack, *Frank Lloyd Wright's Larkin Building: Myth and Fact* (Cambridge, MA: MIT Press, 1987).

——, *Frank Lloyd Wright's Martin House: Architecture as Portraiture* (New York: Princeton Architectural Press, 2004)

Rosenbaum, Alvin, *Usonia: Frank Lloyd Wright's Design for America* (Washington, DC: The Preservation Press, 1993).

Scott, Margaret Helen, *Frank Lloyd Wright's Warehouse in Richland Center, Wisconsin* (Richland Center, WI: Richland County Publishers, 1984).

Sergeant, John, *Frank Lloyd Wright's Usonian Houses: The Case for Organic Architecture* (New York: Whitney Library of Design, 1975).

Smith, Kathryn, *Frank Lloyd Wright: Hollyhock House and Olive Hill* (New York: Rizzoli, 1992).

Sprague, Paul E., ed., *Frank Lloyd Wright and Madison: Eight Decades of Artistic and Social Interaction* (Madison, WI: Elvehjem Museum of Art, University of Wisconsin, 1990).

Storrer, William Allin, *The Architecture of Frank Lloyd Wright: A Complete Catalog,* Third Edition (Chicago: University of Chicago Press, 2002).

Sweeney, Robert L., *Wright in Hollywood: Visions of a New Architecture* (Cambridge, MA: MIT Press, 1994).

Watterson, Kathryn, *Building a Dream: The Sara Smith Story* (Santa Barbara, CA: Smith Publishing Group, 1999).

Wilson, Richard Guy and Sidney K. Robinson, *The Prairie School In Iowa* (Ames, IA: Iowa State University Press, 1977).

Wright, Frank Lloyd, *An Autobiography* (New York: Duell, Sloan, and Pearce, 1943).